Illustrated Sermon Outlines

J. B. Fowler, Jr.

BROADMAN PRESS
Nashville, Tennessee

4222-61
ISBN: 0-8054-2261-7

Dewey Decimal Classification: 251.02
Subject Heading: SERMONS - OUTLINES, SYLLABI, ETC.
Library of Congress Catalog Card Number: 86-2674

Printed in the United States of America

Library of Congress Cataloging-in-Publication Data

Fowler, J. B., 1930-
Illustrated sermon outlines.

1. Sermons—Outlines, syllabi, etc.   2. Homiletical
illustrations.   I. Title.
BV4223.F65 1987   251'.02   86-2674
ISBN 0-8054-2261-7 (pbk.)

Dedication

This book is affectionately dedicated to my parents, Mr. and Mrs. J. B. Fowler, Sr. It was from them that I first learned about Jesus.

Foreword

Illustrated Sermon Outlines is an outstanding collection of sermonic helps, designed to induce creative thought and development on the one hand, while offering superior illustrations and outlines on the other. The treatment of familiar passages is original and fresh. There is enough material given to motivate one toward one's own exegesis and biblical treatment of the great themes presented by the author.

Illustrated Sermon Outlines comes from the prolific reservoir of J. B. Fowler's own pastoral ministry of thirty years, during which time he developed a finely honed style of preaching, which was inspirational, instructional, and poetic. He has carried this same style and sensitivity into the editorship of the *Baptist New Mexican,* a position he has held since 1981. During these years he has become widely read and quoted often throughout the nation in a variety of publications. In demand to fill pulpits in several states, he has been called upon by the Baptist Convention of New Mexico to serve as a seminar leader to teach preaching skills to that state's ministers.

I commend this book to the busy pastor and others who may wish to profit from Dr. Fowler's finely distilled study and research. It will be a practical resource book to use over and again.

W. Winfred Moore, Pastor
First Baptist Church
Amarillo, Texas

Author's Preface

A certain pastor, so the story goes, didn't come home one Sunday night after the evening worship service. But his wife didn't fret about it, because this was nothing unusual.

By midnight she was uneasy, and as the clock in the living room chimed 1 AM, she was nearly beside herself. Calling the police department, she reported that her husband was missing and requested that the police look for him.

It wasn't long until they found him. As though he were in some other world, he was walking down the street, wringing his hands, shaking his head, and mumbling, "Two more next Sunday . . . two more next Sunday!"

The average pastor may preach as many as 156 sermons in a year. To preach this often and to be fresh each time he speaks, is all but an impossible task for a pastor. Having served as a pastor for thirty years, I understand the poor brother who was beside himself because he had "Two more next Sunday."

These illustrated sermon outlines were prepared for busy pastors like him. They were not prepared for the seminary classroom to be dissected, analyzed, pondered, and criticized. They were prepared to help the busy pastor—to give him a few new ideas for next Sunday's sermons.

Space here is inadequate for me to thank all those who encouraged and helped me in the writing of this book. But I must express my gratitude to my secretary, Jana Boley, whose patient typing of this manuscript contributed so much to making the book possible.

Contents

1
A Christian Witness

Scripture: Matthew 5:13-16

Introduction:

In his book *Confessions of a Happy Christian,* Zig Ziglar beautifully demonstrates the power of influence.

A Sunday School teacher named Ezra Kimball led a nineteen-year-old shoe clerk to Christ in 1855. The clerk's name was Dwight L. Moody.

Years later, Moody preached in England in the church served by Dr. Frederick B. Meyer, and Meyer's heart was strangely warmed by the American.

Meyer later came to the United States to preach. In one of the services, a discouraged young preacher named Wilbur Chapman listened to Meyer and was encouraged to stay with the work to which he had been called.

Chapman's ministry grew until he needed an assistant so he selected a young man, a former professional baseball player, who was working at the local YMCA. His name was Billy Sunday.

And in Charlotte, North Carolina, in 1924, Billy Sunday preached with such power that a prayer meeting was started to pray about God's work.

As the group prayed, they asked specifically for God to send another great revival to Charlotte. And God sent Mordecai Ham.

As Mordecai Ham preached in the Charlotte meeting, a sixteen-year-old farm boy came under conviction and was saved. His name was Billy Graham. And Graham has preached to more people than any minister of the gospel in history.

In this passage out of Matthew's Gospel, Jesus underscored

the importance of a Christian's influence. There are two great truths here stated by our Lord.

I. A Christian is to be salt to the world (v. 13).

Jesus, no doubt, meant several things by this expression, for salt was used in a variety of ways.

1. A Christian is to season life.

We are to season the lives of those about us. We are to encourage those who are saved and lead to the Savior those who are lost.

When believers do this, they will keep life from becoming flat and tasteless for those touched.

2. A Christian is to preserve life.

Salt was an important element in the lives of ancient people. To preserve food, the Jews would use salt from the Dead Sea. Salt, worked into the food, kept it from corrupting.

By carefully maintaining our Christian witness, we help preserve sobriety in a nation with more than eleven million alcoholics. We help to preserve morality in a decadent age which dresses immodestly, speaks impurely, marries unscripturally, and lives unchastely.

3. A Christian must not lose his influence.

II. A Christian is to be light to the world (vv. 14-16).

Salt arrests corruption and light dispels ignorance and darkness.

1. A Christian is to reveal the Savior.

Light has several functions and one of them is to reveal. When a darkened room is lighted, all that is in the room is revealed. Christians will reveal the Savior by the lives they live, the words they speak, and the attitudes they have.

2. A Christian is to be a guide to the lost (v. 16).

The Ethiopian eunuch asked Philip in Acts 8:31 how he (the eunuch) could know Jesus "except some man should guide me?" He needed a guide to the Savior just as the world today needs a guide to the Savior.

Conclusion:

When one walks into London's magnificent Westminster Abbey, the first grave one sees is that of Dr. David Livingstone. A missionary, explorer, and physician who served Christ for more than three decades in Africa, Livingstone is buried with England's great heroes.

One of the sweetest memories of David Livingstone's life was the memory of his old Sunday School teacher, David Hogg.

When Hogg was dying, he called the young Livingstone to his bedside and encouraged him to live a life of full, unstinting commitment to Jesus Christ.

"Make religion the everyday business of your life," Hogg told young Livingstone.

History reveals how much Livingstone meant to the kingdom of God. But what will never be known until we get to heaven is how much the Christian witness of David Hogg meant to Livingstone in his formative years.

2
A Fresh Vision of God

Scripture: Isaiah 6:1-13

Introduction:

The late J. R. Glover was a brilliant Cambridge professor. A missionary in China for eighteen years, Glover traveled more than one hundred thousand miles visiting mission stations in the Orient, India, Africa, the Near East, and Latin America. His book, *The Progress of Worldwide Missions,* is a classic in its field and a missions textbook widely used.

Glover tells about watching a Hindu woman in India going through a strange religious exercise. The woman would prostrate herself on the ground, measure her length, and go through the process all over again. In order to travel one mile, Glover related, the woman would prostrate herself more than

800 times. She was journeying toward a place in the Hima-
layas, 1,000 miles away, where a stream of natural gas burned
in the mountains. According to Hindu belief, one of their gods
dwelt in the mountain.

When a Christian missionary asked the woman the reason
for her strange exercise, she said to him in her native tongue,
"Vision of him! Vision of him!"

In this text out of the prophecy of Isaiah, the prophet sought
after and discovered a fresh vision of God. No stranger to God,
Isaiah had faithfully spoken to the people for God during the
reigns of King Jothan, King Ahab, and King Uzziah.

But when King Uzziah died, the heartbroken prophet went
to the Temple to pray. As he prayed, God appeared to him in
a fresh vision, and Isaiah left the Temple to preach to the
people with this fresh vision of God burning in his heart.

In this vision to His prophet, God revealed five distinct characteristics about Himself:

    I. God is the great King (vv. 1-4).
   II. God is the righteous Judge (v. 5).
  III. God is the gracious Redeemer (vv. 6-7).
  IV. God is the commanding Lord (vv. 8-10).
   V. God is the searching Savior (vv. 11-13).

Conclusion:

In his book *We Would See Jesus*, George W. Truett says that
Plato voiced the agelong cry of humankind in these words: "We
look for a God, or a God-inspired man, who will show us our
duty and take away the darkness from our eyes."

Isaiah was such a man. Moved by his fresh vision of God, the
renewed prophet became an evangel for God, sharing that holy
vision with the people to whom he ministered.

3
A Lesson in Prayer

Scripture: Luke 11:1-13

Introduction:

This is not the Lord's Prayer as it is often called. The Lord's Prayer is recorded in John 17. It was prayed by Jesus on the night before He was crucified.

This is the Model Prayer. It is recorded in two places in the Gospels: Matthew 6 and Luke 11.

The prayer was given by Jesus to His disciples at their request. They had come to Jesus, saying, "Lord, teach us to pray." And in response to their request, Jesus gave them a lesson in prayer. By giving it, Jesus was not suggesting that our prayers contain these words alone. Rather, the Lord gave it to His disciples and to us as a guide to fuller and richer praying.

In the prayer, Jesus shows us there are some fundamentals which prayer must contain.

I. There must be reverence in our prayers (v. 2).
"Our Father which art in heaven, hallowed by thy name."

II. There must be priority in our prayers (v. 2).
"Thy kingdom come."

III. There must be submissiveness in our prayers (v. 2).
"Thy will be done, as in heaven, so in earth."

IV. There must be dependence in our prayers (v. 3).
"Give us day by day our daily bread."

V. There must be confession in our prayers (v. 4).
"And forgive us our sins;"

VI. There must be forgiveness in our prayers (v. 4).
"for we also forgive everyone that is indebted to us."

VII. There must be commitment in our prayers (v. 4).

"And lead us not into temptation; but deliver us from evil."

VIII. There must be persistence in our prayers (vv. 5-8).

IX. There must be faith in our prayers (vv. 9-13).

"Ask, and it shall be given you; seek, and ye shall find; knock, and it shall be opened unto you." Each of these is present tense: keep on asking.

Conclusion:

In his moving poem, *Morte d'Arthur* Alfred, Lord Tennyson wrote:

> More things are wrought by prayer
> Than this world dreams of. Wherefore,
>   let thy voice
> Rise like a fountain for me night and
>   day.

Because Jesus knew the importance of prayer, He gave us this lesson to guide us in praying.

4
A Sinner's Plea for Mercy

Scripture: Psalm 51:1-17

Introduction:

Nicolaus Copernicus was born in 1473 and died in 1543. He is the father of modern-day astronomy. He first put forth the theory that the earth is a planet which moves around the sun. It was a courageous theory because the ancient world believed that the sun moved around the earth.

Born in the city of Thorn, Poland, Copernicus, who was also a student of medicine, received his doctor's degree from the University of Ferrara. In Saint John's Church in Thorn is a portrait of Copernicus. Beneath the portrait is an inscription which he wrote:

> I do not ask the grace which thou didst
>   give to St. Paul;
> Nor can I dare to ask the grace thou didst
>   grant to St. Peter;
> But, the mercy thou didst show to the
>   dying robber,
> That mercy show to me.

This was the attitude David possessed when he penned the matchless fifty-first psalm. Like Copernicus, King David made only one request: a plea for mercy.

As we think about a sinner's plea for mercy, consider these thoughts:

I. A guilty heart (vv. 1-3).
   1. A grievous transgression (vv. 1-2; 2 Sam. 11).
   2. A smitten conscience (vv. 1-3; 2 Sam. 12:1-13).

II. A sincere confession (vv. 3-6).
   1. Others cannot be blamed for our sin (v. 3).
   2. Sin cannot forever be hidden (v. 3).
   3. Sin is always against God (v. 4).
   4. God always condemns it (v. 4).
   5. Sin springs from our nature (v. 5).
   6. God honors openness (v. 6).

III. An earnest supplication (vv. 7-12).
   1. A plea for cleansing (v. 7,10).
   2. A plea for spiritual healing (v. 8).
   3. A plea for acceptance (vv. 9,11).
   4. A plea for the return of joy (vv. 8,12).

IV. A sacred vow (vv. 13-17).
   1. To witness by example (v. 13).
   2. To witness by words (vv. 14-15).
   3. To witness by humility (v. 17).

Conclusion:

Passing the buck for sin is as old as humankind. Adam blamed Eve for his transgression. Eve blamed the serpent for her sin. But David blamed no one. He didn't put the blame on Bathsheba or anyone else. David blamed only himself.

Sin is not a pretty word, and it is not readily accepted by our sophisticated generation. In an attempt to excuse themselves of guilt, many twentieth-century wise people refer to sin as "theological fiction" or "a pathological state of mind fomented by the salaried representatives of religion" or "the growing pains of the race." Some call their sin a mistake or a stumble or an erring in good judgment.

But this is all just so much verbal jargon. God condemns and judges sin, and the sinner is left with no alternative, if he wants peace of heart, but to plea for mercy and grace at the hand of God.

5
Answering God's Call

Scripture: Jeremiah 1:4-10

Introduction:

Dr. George Washington Carver, a black scientist who taught for many years at Tuskegee Institute, may have done more for Southern agriculture than any man in history. Born in slavery in Missouri, never knowing his father, Carver fought against terrific odds to make something of his life. It was a constant struggle, but he succeeded as he lived by the motto, "Let down your buckets where you are."

Carver not only made something of himself, but he also gave his life to encouraging others to make the best of what life had given to them.

When Henry Ford offered him $100,000 a year, which was a great deal of money in that day, and the best laboratory money could buy, Carver refused. And when Thomas Edison offered Carver $175,000 a year to work in his laboratory in New Jersey, the humble Christian scientist turned down Edison's offer. He stayed on at Tuskegee Institute where he was paid only $1,500 annually because he felt God was not through with him at

Tuskegee, and that there was still plenty of work Carver could do for Him.

Like the prophet Jeremiah, Carver believed God has a will for every one of us, and that it is our most important business to find and do God's will.

As we consider the matter of answering God's call, let us observe three things that enter into it:

I. The divine will
1. God's will is planned (v. 5).
2. God's will is personal
"I formed thee, . . . I knew thee; . . . I sanctified thee, . . . I ordained thee" (v. 5).
"I shall send thee, . . . I command thee" (v. 7).
"I have put my words in thy mouth" (v. 9).
"I have this day set thee over the nations" (v. 10).

II. The human response
1. It is often fearful (vv. 6,8).
2. It is often faithless (vv. 6-7).

III. The sufficient power
1. It is sufficient to remove our fears (v. 8).
2. It is sufficient to equip us for service (v. 9).

Conclusion:

During the days of the War between the States, General Robert E. Lee sent word to General Stonewall Jackson that he wanted to see him. Sometime soon, Lee indicated, he wanted Jackson to stop by for a talk if he were near.

When Jackson got the message, he rode horseback all night through a storm to meet with General Lee.

When Lee inquired why Jackson had come in such a hurry and through such a bad storm, Jackson replied: "Sir, the least request from my general is a command to me."

God has a will for each of us. And doing God's will is a command which each of us must obey if life is to be full and happy.

6
Are You at Your Wit's End?

Scripture: Psalm 139:1-12

Introduction:

Several years ago, while our family was vacationing in Arkansas, we came upon a peculiar sign on one of the winding roads outside Little Rock. On the sign were printed the words, "Wit's End." And an arrow pointed onward.

We soon discovered the meaning of the sign. Someone who lived in Little Rock, no doubt, had bought a piece of property in those quiet, beautiful hills outside the city and had built a cabin. It was a mountain retreat where he and his family could get away from the racket and tension of city living. And they named their mountain cabin "Wit's End."

There are times when each of us comes to our wit's end. We feel as though we just can't take any more—that we can't go on. Maybe some health problem has debilitated us, or some financial problem has worried us sick. Maybe some family problem has eaten the heart out of us, or some spiritual problem has knocked the breath from us. Whatever the cause, each of us knows—or will know—what it means to come to our wit's end.

One poor, discouraged soul who had come to his wit's end became so disenchanted with life that he wrote in his diary:

> Don't bother me now,
> Don't bother me never;
> I want to be dead
> Forever and ever!

In reading through the Psalms, I found a passage of Scripture that can be of tremendous help to us when we come to our wit's end. I have it marked in my Bible. It is easily found. I can quickly turn to it when I most need it. It has often proved its value.

My special wit's-end passage is Psalm 139. I recommend that you read it when you are at your wit's end.

I. Remember that God knows you (vv. 1-4).
    1. Knows your thoughts (v. 2).
    2. Knows your actions (vv. 2-3).
    3. Knows your words (v. 4).
II. Remember that God loves you (vv. 5-12).
    1. Protecting hand upon you (v. 5).
    2. Protecting presence around you (vv. 7-12).
III. Remember that God guides you (vv. 6,10).
    1. We don't always understand how (v. 6).
    2. He holds our hands (v. 10).

Conclusion:

Sometime ago, I read that some students at a certain university complained they couldn't study because of the noise of the jukebox. So someone installed a silent record, lasting three minutes, in the jukebox. Before the record had been in the jukebox very long, it had to be replaced. The students played it so often that they literally wore it out.

In our noisy kind of world, when we come to our wit's end, let us get alone with God and this psalm. To do so will give each of us a rejuvenating minivacation.

7
Are You Counting on Tomorrow?

Scripture: James 4:13-17

Introduction:

Too many of us are counting on tomorrow. Many are saying, "Tomorrow, we shall be saved"; "Tomorrow, we shall begin to pray"; "Tomorrow, we shall be faithful to Christ"; or, "Tomorrow, we shall do what is right." But tomorrow never comes.

Tomorrow, Raphael would finish his picture. But the picture, half finished, was carried in his funeral procession.

Tomorrow, Charles Dickens would finish his novel. So laying down his pen, he turned his attention elsewhere, and many have wondered how the novel would have ended had the angel of death delayed by a day.

Tomorrow, Franz Schubert would finish his symphony. But Schubert's tomorrow never came, and he left undone his *Unfinished Symphony*.

"Tomorrow, we shall, . . ." wrote Sir Walter Scott in his diary. But this last-written sentence of one of Scotland's greatest writers was never completed. And lovers of literature still wonder what Scott intended to do on the morrow.

Each of these is a striking reminder that tomorrow is the most uncertain, unpredictable friend we have. Of all things uncertain and undependable, none is more uncertain or more undependable than tomorrow.

In the light of this sobering realization, look at what James says about tomorrow:

    I. Plans for tomorrow (vv. 13-14,16).
        1. Are always uncertain (v. 14).
        2. Are often unspiritual (v. 16).
   II. Perils of tomorrow (v. 14).
        1. Lack of knowledge about it.
        2. The brevity of life.
 III. Perjury about tomorrow (vv. 15-17).
        1. Make our will God's will (v. 15).
        2. Act in arrogance, not humility (v. 16).
        3. Such attitudes are evil (v. 17).

Conclusion:

In his book *Macartney's Illustrations*, the late Clarence Macartney tells about a double painting which hangs in the Louvre.

In the first painting, an angry father is ordering his wayward son out of the house. The boy's weeping mother and distressed sisters and brothers stand in the background.

In the second picture, the door of the cottage is open, and the wayward son stands with one foot on the sill and one hand on the door. There is an anguished look on his face. The father lies dead on the bed, and the mother kneels by the side of the bed with her face in her hands.

For the prodigal, the return home was delayed one day too long. His tomorrow was too late.

8
Beauty that Does Not Fade

Scripture: Psalm 90:17a

Introduction:

Many things come in buckets—lard, syrup, honey, paint— and a thousand other things. But, according to an article in *Readers Digest,* beauty also comes in a bucket!

The article, "Beauty by the Bucketful," told about women's never-ending pursuit of loveliness. This feminine craving for beauty, the article declared, has created an American industry which grosses more than seven billion dollars annually.

Beauty by the bucketful means facials, hairdos, makeups, massages, manicures, and pedicures. It means paraffin baths, steam baths, seaweed baths, and mud baths. All of this, the article stated, "is the serious, funny, sad, and somehow charming pursuit of beauty," on the part of the female of the species.

And men, it seems, are also buying beauty by the bucketfuls. Trying to improve on nature's endowments—or lack of them— men are currently spending more than six hundred million dollars a year for perfume, makeup, and night creams!

Men are being told they no longer need to smell like a wet dog, so colognes carrying such intriguing names as "Brut," "Tiger Sweat," "Bathtub Gin," and "Hai Karate" are to be found on the dressing tables of millions of virile, American men.

Beauty by the bucketful—this is the American scene today,

and I would be the last one to discourage the pursuit of it for, as John Keats wrote, "A thing of beauty is a joy forever."

I would, however, remind you of what Solomon said in Proverbs 31:30: "Favour is deceitful, and beauty is vain."

My text speaks about beauty and the pursuit of it. But it does not deal with physical beauty that fades and wanes. Rather, it deals with spiritual beauty—grace, gentleness, and kindness of life which the Lord Jesus gives to them who walk in intimate fellowship with Him. It is a beauty which does not fade.

Let me suggest to you that:

I. This beauty should be sought.
   1. Because it is inward beauty (1 Pet. 3:3-4).
   2. Because it is precious beauty (1 Pet. 3:4).
II. This beauty can be lost.
   1. When sin enters, this beauty fades (Ps. 51:7).
   2. When joy goes, this beauty fades (Ps. 51:8,12).
   3. When the spirit is wrong, this beauty fades (Ps. 51:6,10).
III. This beauty cannot be bought.
   1. Money can't buy it (1 Pet. 1:18).
   2. The blood of Jesus purchases it (1 Pet. 1:18-19).
IV. This beauty has to be wrought.
   1. It is the gift of God (Eph. 2:8-9).
   2. It expresses itself in Christlike character (Gal. 5:22-23; Rom. 8:29; 1 John 3:2).
   3. It is produced by the Holy Spirit (Gal. 5:22-23; Eph. 5:9).

Conclusion:

We are told in Psalm 96:6 where we shall find this beauty of our Lord: "Strength and beauty are in his sanctuary."

What does the psalmist mean? He means that one will find God's beauty in the quiet place of prayer, communion, and meditation. We will not have the beauty of the Lord our God upon us unless we seek Him, follow Him, and walk with Him.

There is a beauty that does not fade. It is found in trusting Jesus and walking with Him. And it is a beauty that will grow with the passing of time and eternity.

9
Bought and Paid For

Scripture: *1 Corinthians 6:19-20*

Introduction:
In his book *Don't Disappoint God,* R. L. Middleton relates that the little dauphin Charles, who was the son of King Louis XVI and Marie Antoinette, was the heir to the French throne.

After the surly mob had slain the king and the queen, the mob wanted to kill Prince Charles. But through the influence of one man, the prince was spared to be turned over to "Old Meg," the vilest woman in Paris, who would leave no stone unturned to ruin the character of the prince.

But Prince Charles resisted "Old Meg's" evil influence, and at times when she would curse and swear at the prince with the vilest words, insisting that he repeat her words, the little dauphin would grit his teeth and shout, "I will not say it! I was born to be a king."

We believers have been bought and paid for by Jesus Christ. We were born again to be kings and queens unto Him. As Paul said in this passage, "Ye are not your own."

As we remember who we are and what price has been paid to redeem us from our sins, Paul told us several things we need to remember.
- I. The Christian and his body
  - 1. Our body is not our own (v. 19).
  - 2. Our body is the temple of the Holy Spirit (v. 19).
- II. The price paid to redeem us
  - 1. We have been bought (v. 20).
    Bought is from a verb which means to buy in the marketplace.
  - 2. The price paid (v. 20).

Paul did not state the price paid, but Peter did in 1 Peter 1:18-19.
III. The responsibility that is now ours
Paul used "therefore" to show us our new responsibility (v. 20).
1. We are to glorify God (v. 20).
2. God is to be Lord of our lives (v. 20).
"In your body, and in your spirit."

Conclusion:

When Alfred, Lord Tennyson, the great English poet, was asked what his dearest wish was, Tennyson replied, "A clear vision of God."

When we believers have a clearer vision of God and the price He has paid in Christ to redeem us, we will respond by laying all we are and have in love upon His altar.

10
Christ, Our Sacrifice

Scripture: *Romans 5:6-11*

Introduction:

After the Germans were defeated in World War I, Crown Prince Wilhelm, the eldest son of Kaiser Wilhelm, offered himself as a hostage to save some of his people.

After Germany fell, the Kaiser's family fled to neutral Holland for safety. From there, the crown prince wrote King George V of Great Britain, offering to give himself as a hostage if Britain would spare 900 Germans who were wanted as war criminals.

In the letter to the king, young Wilhelm wrote:

> As a former heir to the throne of my German fatherland,
> I am willing to offer myself on behalf of my compatriots in
> this fateful hour. . . . If the allied and associated govern-

ments require a sacrifice let them take me instead of the 900 Germans whose only fault was that they served their fatherland in the war.

Although the prince was never called upon to give himself as a sacrifice for his people, the 900 Germans were never brought to trial.

The sacrificial offer of Germany's crown prince was a praiseworthy gesture that cost him nothing. But the sacrifice which Jesus Christ, the Prince of glory, offered for mankind, cost Him everything.

Paul discussed Christ, our Sacrifice, in this text of Scripture.

  I. The One who sacrificed.
     1. He is identified as the "Christ" (vv. 6,8).
       Christ translates the Hebrew word *anointed*. It identifies Him as the Messiah. It is used twenty-five times in Acts alone in the messianic sense.
     2. He is identified as "his Son" (v. 10).
       Jesus is called "son of Joseph" in Luke 3:23 and 4:22; "son of Mary" in Mark 6:3; "Son of David"—a messianic title—in Matthew, Mark, and Luke; "Son of man" in all the Gospels—always used by Jesus and never by others; but in this text He is called "his Son"—referring to Almighty God. John shows us clearly who this Son is in John 3:16.

 II. The ones for whom He sacrificed.
     Notice the downward progression:
     1. He died for those "without strength" (v. 6).
       It means the sick, diseased, infirm—those with no moral or spiritual goodness.
     2. He died for "the ungodly" (v. 6).
       It means those who are impious, who have no reverential awe of God.
     3. He died for "sinners" (v. 8).
       It means those devoted to sin, preeminently sinful, especially wicked. (See Rom. 3:10-18).
     4. He died for "enemies" (v. 10).
       It describes those who are obnoxious to divine pleasure, turned against God, and displeasing to God.

Although we were without moral or spiritual strength, impious and irreverent toward God, devoted to sin and preeminently sinful, and obnoxious to the divine pleasure, still God loved us and Christ sacrificed for us.

III. The reasons for the sacrifice.

Paul listed four of them.

1. As a demonstration of the divine love (v. 8).
2. To justify us (v. 9).
3. To reconcile us to God (v. 10).
4. To save us from God's wrath (v. 9).

Conclusion:

In his book *Paul and Rabbinic Judaism,* W. D. Davis gives some interesting facts about the sacrifices which were offered for centuries in the Temple at Jerusalem. Davis deals only with the official sacrifices, not the private sacrifices offered by worshipers.

In a year, he says, 1,093 lambs were sacrificed, 113 bulls, 37 rams, and 32 goats.

But each of these sacrifices in the Temple pointed to God's sacrifice for sin which would be made in the fullness of time. When Christ became our sacrifice on Calvary, He fulfilled and validated all the sacrifices ever offered on Jewish altars.

And today, Christ alone is our sacrifice for sin.

11
Consider Christ

Scripture: *Matthew 16:13-16*

Introduction:

In his book *Iron Shoes,* Roy Angell tells about an old Confederate soldier who was admiring the statue of General Robert E. Lee astride his horse Traveller. The magnificent monument stands on Monument Street in Richmond.

As the old soldier stood admiring the statue of the general

with whom he had served during the War Between the States, he said to a passerby who was standing near:

> I have looked at it in the early morning with the sun rising behind it, and it was beautiful. I have looked at it in the evening with the sun setting behind it, and it was beautiful. I have looked at it with the James River as a background, and it was beautiful. I have laid beside the riger and looked up at it silhouetted against the sky, and it was beautiful. From no one position could you possibly see and appreciate all its glory.[1]

Many of us say that about Jesus. To know Christ as one's Savior and to walk in fellowship with Him is our greatest privilege.

As we consider Christ in this brief outline, look at these truths about Him:

I. He was born miraculously.
    1. He was divinely conceived (Matt. 1:20).
    2. He was born of a virgin (Matt. 1:23).
II. He lived sinlessly.
    1. He said this of Himself (John 8:29).
    2. Others said it of Him (1 Pet. 2:22).
    3. No one ever accused Him of sin (John 8:46).
III. He died vicariously.
    Webster defines vicarious as, "substituted or performed in the place of another."
    1. He is our substitute (1 Pet. 3:18).
    2. He died to save us (John 1:29; 1 Pet. 1:18-20).
IV. He was raised triumphantly.
    1. He spoke of His resurrection (Matt. 12:38-41).
    2. It is the heart of the gospel (1 Cor. 15:1-5,13-23).

Conclusion:

It was said that Julian, "the Apostate," a Roman emperor who was an enemy of Christianity, tried to restore pagan religion to the Roman Empire.

But in AD 362 when he invaded Persia, Julian turned to one of his soldiers who was a Christian and asked him what he supposed Jesus was doing that day.

The soldier answered that since Jesus was a carpenter He

might have taken the day off from building mansions in heaven to build a coffin for the emperor.

And, so the story relates, Julian fell in battle that day and died within a few hours. But shortly before he died, he took a fistful of dust that was clotted with his own blood, and throwing it toward heaven he shouted, "Oh, Galilean, thou hast conquered!"[2]

Indeed, He is the conquering Christ.

1. Roy C. Angell, *Iron Shoes* (Nashville: Broadman Press, 1953), p. 56.

2. For this and other illustations from history see my *Living Illustrations* (Nashville: Broadman Press, 1985), p. 24.

12
Coping with Life's Interruptions

Scripture: Genesis 37:28

Introduction:

I'm thinking of two young men. For each life was interrupted when they were young and when their futures seemed so bright. One of the men was Thomas Alva Edison, who became America's greatest inventor.

One day when Edison was just a boy, he was experimenting with phosphorus on a moving train when the phosphorus burst into flames and set the car on fire. The conductor slapped Edison on the ears and threw him off the train. Edison said later that when the conductor hit him he felt something snap inside his head, and his deafness started from that time.

In later life Edison became almost totally deaf, but he said he didn't mind so much because it helped him to concentrate.

Although his life was interrupted by the thoughtless act of the conductor, the interruption brought a blessing.

The other young man was Joseph, the son of Jacob. Sent one day to check on his brothers who were tending sheep on the plains of Dothan, the jealous brothers sold young Joseph to some Midianite traders for twenty pieces of silver.

But before God was through with Joseph, He used the interruption that could have destroyed Joseph to open doors for him in Egypt that never would have opened otherwise.

Life may be and often is interrupted by a thousand different things. Some are good, and some are bad. But when life's interruptions come, we need to learn how to cope with them so that God can use them for His glory and our good.

    I. Life's interruptions may mock us (Ps. 105:17-18; Gen. 37:18-28).
        1. They may try us.
        2. They can break us.
    II. Life's interruptions may mellow us.
        1. They can teach us to handle our pride (Gen. 37:3-8).
        2. They can teach us to handle our temptations (Gen. 39:7-12).
        3. They can teach us to live humbly (Gen. 42:21-24; 45:1-5).
        4. They can teach us to see God's hand at work (Gen. 45:7).
   III. Life's interruptions may make us.
        Helen Keller once said about her blindness and deafness: "I thank God for my handicaps, for through them I have found myself, my work, and my God."
        1. They can prepare us for greater service (Gen. 39:21-23).
        2. They can open doors for us that would never open otherwise (Gen. 41:41-46).

Conclusion:

Thomas Edison was almost deaf and had no more than three months of formal schooling. But his handicap proved to be his greatest blessing.

Phillips Brooks was a peerless New England preacher. But Brooks didn't want to be a preacher, he wanted to teach school. But when schoolteaching didn't work out for him, he turned to the ministry and found his life's work.

James Whistler wanted to be a soldier, but he flunked out of

West Point. Turning to painting, he immortalized himself with his striking portrait titled *Whistler's Mother.*

Booker T. Washington, born a Negro slave, coped with his hindrances and handicaps and became the greatest educator among black people America has known. Frequently, Washington spoke about "the advantages of disadvantages."

History is filled with the biographies of people whose lives were interrupted by one thing or the other. But, learning to cope with life's interruptions, they lived nobly and successfully.

13
Dealing with
Discouragements

Scripture: **2 Kings 13:14-19**

Introduction:

Every year the women of Liberal, Kansas, compete with the women of Olney, England, in what is called the "pancake race." At the end of the street down which the English women run, there is a red brick house where the author of one of our best-loved hymns lived from 1767 through 1786. His name was William Cowper.

Several years ago a survey was taken in Australia, Canada, Great Britain, and the United States, and the question was asked, "What is your favorite hymn?"

When the answers came back, it was discovered that one of William Cowper's hymns was among the top one hundred favorite hymns of the English-speaking world.

> There is a fountain filled with blood
> Drawn from Immanuel's veins;
> And sinners plunged beneath that flood,
> Lose all their guilty stains.

At a certain time in his life, William Cowper fought a terrible battle with depression. In fact, he tried to commit suicide on more than one occasion. But in moments when his faith was strong, he produced some of the greatest Christian hymns and poetry we have.

Other than the hymn just mentioned, perhaps Cowper is best known for his lines:

> God moves in a mysterious way
> His wonders to perform;
> He plants his footsteps in the sea
> And rides upon the storm.

Discouragement is a common problem that attacks the rich and poor, the weak and the mighty, the king and the pauper, and the young and the old. Even biblical characters were not immune to discouragement.

Our Scripture text reveals that when young King Joash came to visit the old, dying prophet Elisha, the young king was terribly discouraged. The mighty army of Syria had waited for the young and inexperienced king to come to the throne. It was coiled, like a huge serpent, ready to strike Israel and destroy the nation.

Not knowing what to do, young Joash went to see the eighty-year-old prophet Elisha. Desperate, King Joash asked what he should do in the face of such discouragement.

Notice, now, in this passage of Scripture, how the prophet instructed the young king to deal with his discouragement. And as we study Elisha's example to Joash, we shall gain some valuable lessons in how to deal with our own discouragement.

I. Submit fully (vv. 14-16).
  1. Our strength to cope is insufficient (v. 14).
  2. The Lord will show us how to cope (vv. 15-16).
II. Act immediately (vv. 17-18).
  1. Do as God tells us (v. 17).
  2. Do it without questioning (vv. 17-18).
III. Believe strongly (vv. 18-19).
  1. Seek the divine counsel in faith (v. 18).
  2. Act upon it (vv. 18-19).
IV. Persist doggedly (vv. 18-19).
  1. Don't give up (v. 18).
  2. Keep at it (v. 19).

Conclusion:

Dr. Norman Vincent Peale is one of America's most popular preachers. Shortly after he had written his book *The Power of Positive Thinking,* during the early days of his ministry, Peale was severely criticized by other ministers who called him more of a psychologist than a preacher.

Peale was so crushed by the criticism that he seriously considered resigning as pastor of the Marble Collegiate Church in New York City. In fact, as he was riding a train to visit his father who was critically ill, Peale wrote out his letter of resignation.

When he shared his discouragement with his father, who was also a minister, the elder Peale couldn't talk because of his affliction. Therefore, he communicated with his son through gestures. But Norman didn't tell his father about his intention to resign.

A few days after the elder Peale died, Norman's mother gave him a letter which his father had written. In the letter, his father said something like this: "Don't be discouraged by what other ministers say. You are preaching the gospel as it ought to be preached. Don't quit!"

That note saved the ministry of Dr. Peale, and millions of people around the world have been blessed and encouraged by his ministry. Perhaps more than anyone in his day, Peale has helped people deal with their discouragement.

14
Dealing with Sin in the Church

Scripture: 1 Corinthians 5:1-13

Introduction:

During the First World War an unknown British soldier supposedly wrote the following lines:

> The padre 'e says I'm a sinner,
> John Bull 'e says I'm a saint,
> Both of 'em bound to be liars
> I'm neither of them, I ain't.
> I'm a man, and a man is a mixture
> Right down from the day of his birth
> Where a part of 'im come from Heaven
> And a part of 'im come from earth.[1]

The British soldier did a good job of summing up the dual nature of believers. We were born with a sinful nature, and it constantly pulls us toward evil. But when we are saved, we are given the divine nature, and it constantly pulls us toward God. From conversion until death, these two natures wrestle for control of us. And the life we live reveals to which of the two natures we listen.

The struggle believers have with these two natures was a constant problem at Corinth. Many of the believers had only recently been saved and pulled out of paganism. And when they came into the church, many of them brought their sins with them, poisoning the body of Christ. Paul, therefore, wrote the church and told it to deal with the unrepentant sinners who were living according to their sinful natures, and poisoning the fellowship of believers.

As I see it, there are three emphases pertaining to this in this chapter.

   I. The problem of sin in the church.
      1. Sometimes immorality is a problem (v. 1).
      2. Sometimes pride is a problem (v. 2).
  II. The neglect of discipline in the church.
      1. The discipline of unrepentant sinners is scriptural (vv. 2b,4-5,7,9,11).
      2. The discipline of unrepentant sinners must be redemptive (v. 5).
      3. The discipline of unrepentant sinners is commanded (v. 9-11,13).
 III. The precious purity of the church.
      1. Impurities in the church affect the whole body (v. 6).
      2. Impurities in the church are incompatible with the purity of Christ (v. 7).

Conclusion:

This is not a very enjoyable passage to read because it deals with matters we would rather not face. But the church is the bride of Jesus Christ, and she is to be kept holy and pure for Him. The church sins against Her Savior and lover when she refuses to deal with the problem of sin in her midst.

But until the church rediscovers the scriptural teaching of discipline in the church, she will not rediscover the power that rested upon the church in the first century.

---

1. Quoted in Roy C. Angell, *Baskets of Silver* (Nashville: Broadman Press), pp. 40-41. Out of print.

15
Do You Need a Miracle?

Scripture: Luke 5:12-15

Introduction:

Sometimes facetiously, sometimes in dead earnestness, we hear someone say, "What I need is a miracle!"

A student, dreading a calamitous verdict on a final exam, sighs, "What I need is a miracle!"

A young man, broke and without any means of earning money for his big Saturday night date, pessimistically exclaims, "What I need is a miracle!"

A father, facing a problem that is mountainous, prays, "Lord, I need a miracle!"

And a mother, with a desperately sick child who has been given no hope by the physician, humbly bows her head by the side of the child, sobbing, "Please, Lord Jesus, I need a miracle!"

The host at the wedding at Cana in Galilee needed a miracle. The wine was exhausted, and he faced the embarassment of being remembered as a poor host. Mary turned to Jesus on his behalf (John 2:1-11).

The man who had been crippled thirty-eight years and who lay at Bethesda's pool waiting to be healed, needed a miracle.

Martha and Mary, grieving over Lazarus their dead brother, needed a miracle that only Jesus could perform.

And the poor, helpless leper of this passage, an outcast from society, needed the miracle of healing that only Jesus could bring.

I. The request.

He makes but one request of Jesus: "Lord, if thou wilt, thou canst make me clean" (v. 12).

1. Let us ask out of a sense of need (v. 12).

The verse says the "man [was] full of leprosy" (v. 12).

2. Let us go directly to Jesus.

In a sermon preached on the "Baptist Hour" many years ago, Dr. H. H. Hobbs said: "The Jews believed only God could cure leprosy. This explains why this man knelt before Jesus. He regarded Him as God." Probably some of Jesus' disciples were with Him, but the Bible says the man went straight to Jesus: "who seeing Jesus fell on his face, and besought him" (v. 12).

"Seeing" is in the aorist tense: fixed his eyes upon Jesus. "Fell on his face" is also aorist: he fell down immediately into this fixed position.

3. Let us ask earnestly.

"And besought him" (v. 12). The aorist tense shows determination.

"Saying" is in the present tense: He kept on saying. He was earnest because he needed a miracle. This was his chance, and he wouldn't miss it! (See Jas. 5:16.)

II. The response.

The leper made his request and waited for the Lord's response. There was nothing more the man could do.

1. Christ will respond personally.

"And he put forth his hand, and touched him, saying, I will: be thou clean" (v. 13).

"He" is middle voice: "He, Himself, touched him!" There was no proxy involved.

2. Christ will respond immediately.

The answer may not come immediately, but Christ's personal response, His comforting presence, and grace will be given immediately (v. 13).

In this instance, Christ's whole response was immediate: "He put forth his hand" (v. 13). It is the aorist tense: immediately. "And touched him" (v. 13). It is the aorist tense—immediately.

"Be thou clean" (v. 13). It is the aorist tense—immediately. And Luke adds: "Immediately the leprosy departed from him" (v. 13).

3. Christ will respond as He wills.

"And he put forth his hand, and touched him, saying, I will" (v. 13). "Will" is in the aorist tense: "I am willing now!"

III. The result.

Other than his healing, what resulted from the man's encounter with Christ? When our prayers are answered, what results should be obvious in our lives?

1. We ought to rejoice.

Verse 15 indicates that the man so rejoiced in his miracle that it affected "great multitudes."

2. We ought to be a better witness.

The man's testimony brought multitudes to Jesus who were also healed by Him (v. 15).

3. We ought to be more obedient.

Jesus gave the leper three things to do, none of which, apparently, he did:

"And he charged him to tell no man: but go, and show thyself to the priest, and offer for thy cleansing, according as Moses commanded" (v. 14).

4. We ought to use it to glorify God.

Jesus instructed him to "tell no man." He told the leper to glorify God by showing himself to the priest and by offering a sacrifice as Moses commanded. He was to glorify God, not by spreading the word through the whole city but by being obedient (vv. 14-15).

Conclusion:

In *Aurora Leigh,* Elizabeth Barrett Browning wrote:

> Earth's crammed with heaven,
> And every common bush afire
> with God.

Just being alive is a miracle. In reality, earth is crammed with all kinds of miracles. When we have a great need or a heavy burden or a grieving heart, we ought to take our burden to the Lord and in faith expect a miracle from Him.

16
Facing Life Courageously

Scripture: *The Book of Habakkuk*

Introduction:

When the SS *Dorchester* sank in the North Atlantic in 1943 during World War II, four chaplains went down with the ship: a Catholic priest, a Jewish rabbi, and two Protestant ministers.

One of the young chaplains was Clark Poling, the son of Dr. Daniel A. Poling who was Norman Vincent Peale's predecessor at the Marble Collegiate Church in New York City.

After the torpedo struck the ship, it was discovered that four of the enlisted men on board did not have life preservers. The chaplains took off their life preservers and gave them to the four enlisted men. As the survivors rowed away from the rapidly sinking ship, the last scene they saw on deck was the four chaplains, with their arms around each other, kneeling together in prayer.

Robert Schuller, well-known American television preacher and pastor of the Crystal Cathedral in California, says he asked Dr. Poling how he kept his sanity during those days shortly after his chaplain son died. Poling told Schuller that it was hard, and that often he was unable to pray.

But Poling added that, for the longest time after his son's death, every morning upon arising, he would go to his east window, look at the daylight breaking in the east, and say three times out loud, "I believe! I believe! I believe!"

Life may not be easy for us, but we must face it with courage. Even when we don't understand why things are as they are, still we have to believe and face life courageously.

This is where Habakkuk found himself. When it was revealed to him that his beloved Judah would be invaded by the Babylonians, Habakkuk was troubled. He didn't understand why God would punish the Jews for their sins by using a people much more wicked than they were. He had been reared to believe that God is good, just, and righteous. But what Habakkuk saw around him and what had been revealed to him about Judah's future, caused Habakkuk to ask some hard questions. Habakkuk directed his questions *to* God—not against Him. Listening to the voice of God, he waited until the answer came before drawing his final conclusions about the goodness and justice of God. He learned that, although evil may prosper for a while, the righteous alone have a permanent blessing.

In spite of what Habakkuk understood, and did not understand, he faced life courageously and left a good example for us to follow.

Although many things could be shared from this book, there are four simple statements I want you to see:

    I. The problems that face us (1:2-4, 12-17).
    II. The promises that sustain us (1:5-11).
    III. The providence that strengthens us (2:1-5).
    IV. The peace that surrounds us (3:17-19).

Conclusion:

When Abraham Lincoln left Springfield, Illinois, for the White House, the burden of his new office lay heavily upon his shoulders. Addressing his friends in Springfield, Lincoln said, "Without divine assistance I cannot succeed; with it I cannot fail."

Lincoln, like Habakkuk, had come to a place in life where his wisdom, understanding, and strength were totally inadequate. But he drew upon the divine wisdom and resources that never fail. And, as Lincoln faced his difficult task courageously, so did Habakkuk the prophet.

That's the secret for us in our day. Though we do not understand life, and even some of the ways God deals with us, we must believe in Him and serve Him courageously and faithfully.

17
Facing the Future Unafraid

Scripture: *Exodus 13:17-22*

Introduction:

If the people who make up the average Sunday morning congregation were to be asked the question, "What is your greatest fear?" what would be their answers?

I think some of them would say, "My greatest fear is ill health." But others would reply, "My greatest fear is loneliness." And some would say, "My greatest fear is the failure of my business."

But if someone were to keep a tally sheet and reduce our greatest fears to their basic element, I think most of us would reply, "I am most afraid of the future."

The text for this message comes from the history of Israel. For 430 years the Jews had been captives in Egypt. Now they were moving out through the wilderness toward the land flowing with milk and honey—the land God had promised them.

But the Jews were just common folks like you and me. And as they left the security of Egypt, which they had known all their lives, and faced the trackless wilderness and the journey into a land about which they knew very little, they must have been afraid.

No believer knows the future. But we know Him who holds the future in His hands. Therefore, there is no need to fear what tomorrow may bring.

This text gives us some suggestions as to what we can do to face the future unafraid. Look at each of them:
I. Wait for God's time (v. 17).
  1. God's timing is best (v. 17).
  2. God will make a way (v. 17).
II. Follow God's leadership (vv. 17-18,21-22).
  1. He will go with us (vv. 18,21-22).
  2. God knows the best way (vv. 17-18).
III. Believe God's promises (v. 19).
  1. Their fulfillment may be delayed (v. 19).
  2. Their fulfillment will come (v. 19).

Conclusion:
Beethoven, when told at age forty-two that he was going deaf, courageously replied, "Then I will take life by the throat!"

General William Booth, the great Christian who founded the Salvation Army, was told he was going blind. Booth's courageous reply was: "I have used my sight for the glory of God, now I will use my blindness for His glory!"

When John Bunyan, author of *The Pilgrim's Progress,* was thrown into prison at Bedford, England, for preaching the gospel, Bunyan relied: "I will stay in this dungeon until moss grows on my eyes."

God expects Christians to face the future unafraid. And the examples of great believers through the centuries testify that it can be done.

18
From Fear to Faith

Scripture: Psalm 73:1-5,12-14,23-28

Introduction:
Perhaps Alfred, Lord Tennyson's best-known poem is "In Memoriam." When his friend Arthur Henry Hallam died in

1833, Tennyson was deeply grieved. He didn't understand why his young friend had to die. For the next seventeen years he wrestled with these questions, putting his thoughts down in one of his best-loved poems. Seventeen years later, in 1850, he finished "In Memoriam."

> Forgive my grief for one removed,
>   Thy creature, whom I found so fair.
> I trust he lives in thee, and there
>   I find him worthier to be loved.
>
> Forgive these wild and wandering cries,
>   Confusions of a wasted youth;
> Forgive them where they fail in truth,
>   And in thy wisdom make me wise.
>
> ....
>
> I hold it true, whate'er befall;
>   I feel it, when I sorrow most;
> 'Tis better to have loved and lost
>   Than never to have loved at all.

For several years Tennyson's faith faltered. But after the clouds of uncertainty lifted from him, it seems his faith was stronger than before.

As the author of Psalm 73 surveyed the condition of Israel, and as he witnessed the wicked prospering on every hand while the righteous seemed barely to get by, his faith faltered. However, God led him through his personal darkness and out into the glorious light of a rediscovered faith.

In looking at this psalm, I discover it is a realistic commentary on life.

I. A faltering faith (vv. 1-5,7-9,13-14).
   1. Faith may falter during difficult times (v. 2).
   2. Faith will falter beneath the burden of self-pity (vv. 3-5,7-9,13-14).
II. A rewarding faith (vv. 23-28).
   1. The righteous have an eternal presence (vv. 23-24, 28).
   2. The righteous have an eternal guide (v. 24).
   3. The righteous have an eternal reward (vv. 24-25).

Conclusion:

Fridtjof Nansen was a Norwegian polar explorer who was

born in 1861 and died in 1930. He also served as the Norwegian delegate to the League of Nations after the close of World War I.

On one of his trips to the Arctic, Nansen's crew let down a sounding line to calculate the depth of the water. The water was so deep that the crew added more and more line until finally there was no more line to be added. Still not knowing the depth of the water, Nansen recorded in his logbook, "Thirty-five hundred fathoms—and deeper than that."

When our faith falters under some sorrow or crisis, will the grace of God be sufficient for us?

And millions answer, "Yes, His grace is greater than all our needs."

19
Gifts of Grace

Scripture: *Romans 5:1-5*

Introduction:

John Newton wrote the hymn "Amazing Grace," one of the best-loved hymns of Christendom.

In London's Church of Saint Mary Woolnoth, one can read John Newton's inscription:

JOHN NEWTON, Clerk,
Once an infidel and libertine;
A servant of slaves in Africa:
Was by the rich mercy of our Lord and Saviour
Jesus Christ,
Preserved, restored, pardoned,
And appointed to preach the Faith
He had long laboured to destroy.
Near sixteen years at Olney in Bucks,
And twenty-seven years in this church.

John Newton was the son of a seaman. And in adult life, Newton was the captain of his own ship.

Publicly flogged and disgraced for having lost his ship at sea, Newton went to Africa to work for a man who dealt in slaves. Eventually, Newton became the captain of his own slave ship, which he named the *Jesus.*

Converted at the age of twenty-three, Newton decided at forty that God had called him to preach. Accepted as an Anglican clergyman, Newton became curate at Olney in Buckinghamshire in 1764. And during the years he served there, he wrote the hymn for which he is best remembered:

> Amazing grace, how sweet the sound,
> That saved a wretch like me!
> I once was lost, but now am found,
> Was blind, but now I see.

Writing out of his own experience, Newton penned the third stanza:

> Thr' many dangers, toils, and snares,
> I have already come;
> 'Tis grace hath bro't me safe thus far,
> And grace will lead me home.

In Romans 5 Paul wrote out of his own experience of having walked in the grace of Jesus Christ. Reminding the Roman Christians that they were saved by the grace of God and that they continue to be blessed by that grace, Paul declared: "By whom also we have access by faith into this grace wherein we stand" (v. 2).

In these verses, Paul wrote of the gifts of grace which the Heavenly Father gives to each of His children.

I. We have right standing with God (v. 1).
II. We have peace with God (v. 1).
III. We have access to God (v. 2).
IV. We have hope in God (v. 2).
V. We have victory through God (vv. 3-4).
VI. We have the love of God (v. 5).

Conclusion:

In a 1980 edition of *Proclaim* magazine, I read about Paul Staggs of Little Rock, Arkansas, who won a $250 jackpot.

Staggs won the money by matching the winning numbers in his copy of the "Shoppers News."

But Staggs wasn't the only one who was a winner. Thirty-nine thousand other readers also won because a printing mistake was made in the paper.

But there is no mistake about this: every sinner who receives the grace of God is a winner. By grace he wins over sin, and through grace he wins a right standing with God, peace with God, access to God, hope in God, victory through God, and the love of God.

20
God's Greatest Promise

Scripture: John 5:24

Introduction:
Hudson Pope, in a *1960 Keswick Week* book, told about a farmer who became seriously ill and thought he was going to die. Praying earnestly that God would spare his life, the farmer promised God that if He would let him live, he would sell his best calf and give the money to the Lord's work.

The farmer recovered and quickly forgot his promise. But the Lord reminded him of the vow in a strange way.

One evening as the farmer was going to the village church to hear a visiting speaker, he came to the door of the church just as the choir was singing "I have heard of a beautiful city."

As he reached to open the door, the choir came to the chorus where the joyous statement is made, "The half has never been told."

But the farmer misunderstood the sentence. He understood the choir to sing, "The calf has never been sold."

He never attended that service. Turning around and rushing home, the farmer immediately set in motion plans to sell the calf he had promised to God.

The Bible is a Book of divine promises. And every promise God has made in His Word, He will keep. He has committed Himself to the keeping of His promises.

But this passage in John's Gospel reveals to us God's greatest promise. It is the promise of everlasting life to all who will accept Jesus Christ as their Savior.

I. The credibility of the promise (v. 24).
  1. It is a promise that is dependable.
     "Verily, verily, I say unto you."
     It means, "truly, truly." Jesus used this word twice to emphasize the dependability of the thing of which He spoke.
  2. It is a promise from Jesus.
     Notice the one who gives the promise: "I say unto you." The credibility of any promise depends on the one who makes it. And it is impossible for Jesus to lie because He is truth (John 14:6; Titus 1:2).

II. The conditions of the promise (v. 24).
     Some of God's promises and blessings are without condition. But there are two conditions to receiving this promise.
  1. One must hear the Word.
     The word *hear* means more than to hear with the ears. The word means "to attend to; consider; understand; perceive by the ear what is announced to one's hearing."
  2. One must believe on Jesus.
     "Believeth on him that sent me." To believe on Him who has sent Christ is to believe on Christ. It is to accept the testimony the Father has given that Jesus is the Christ, His Son. It is to accept the testimony of the Father that He has sent Jesus into the world to save us from our sins. But it is not head belief. It is heart belief.

III. The guarantees in the promise (v. 24).
     A promise is worthless unless it is binding. Here the Heavenly Father binds Himself to three things.
  1. He guarantees everlasting life.
  2. He guarantees the immediate removal of condemnation.

The tense of the verb *passed* indicates that the believer has passed out of spiritual death into spiritual life, with the result that one is still in that spiritual life.

3. He guarantees the immediate gift of everlasting life.

"Hath [present tense] everlasting life."

Conclusion:

Someone once asked Confederate General Robert E. Lee's aide about a certain thing that the general had promised.

"What guarantee do I have that the general will do what he has promised?" the doubter asked.

Lee's aide promptly replied, "You have General Lee's promise. You could have no better guarantee."

21
Heaven's Best for Earth's Worst

Scripture: 1 Corinthians 13

Introduction:

According to Henry Drummond, love is the greatest thing in the world. And who of us would disagree?

The church at Corinth was missing and neglecting the greatest thing in the world. Divided by pride and quarrelings, they were debating the question: "What is the greatest of the spiritual gifts?"

One faction within the church said, "The gift of wisdom is the greatest Christian gift." But they were rebuked by another element which answered, "No, the greatest virtue a Christian can possess is knowledge." Still others were giving different answers to the question. Some were saying it was faith; others were saying it was the working of a miracle; while others were saying it was the gift of prophecy or the ability to speak in tongues or to interpret tongues.

Paul set them all straight in chapter 13 as he showed them and us that heaven's best gift for earth's worst is Christian love.

I. The necessity of love (vv. 1-3).
   1. More important than eloquence (v. 1).
   2. More important that the spectacular gifts (v. 2).
   3. More important than faith (v. 2).
   4. More important than sacrifice (v. 3).
II. The characteristics of love (vv. 4-7).
   1. What love is not.
      It is not envious; it is not haughty; it is not vainglorious; it is not discourteous; it is not selfish; it is not irritable; it is not retaliative; and it is not indifferent.
   2. What love is.
      Love is patience; love is kindness; love is courtesy; and love is unselfishness.
III. The permanence of love (vv. 8-13).
   1. Prophecies shall pass away.
   2. Tongues shall cease.
   3. Knowledge shall vanish.
   4. But love endures.

Conclusion:

In the Garden of Eden, Adam and Eve discovered both earth's best and its worst. When they sinned, a stream of poison began flowing from Eden that has encircled and infected the world.

But at the cross the Heavenly Father presented heaven's best gift for earth's worst blight. And the love which Christ demonstrated on the cross He has given to believers to demonstrate to the earth.

When the sun rises and sets no more; when the light of the moon has been extinguished; when the stars have fallen from the heavens; and when the fragrance of earth's flowers has been overcome by the fiery breath of God's judgment blast, love will be as brilliant, as permanent, and as fragrant as ever.

And in heaven it shall be sweeter and nobler than we have ever known it on earth.

22
Help from on High

Scripture: Psalm 121

Introduction:

James A. Garfield was the twentieth president of the United States. Inaugurated in 1881, Garfield was shot the following July by Charles J. Guiteau. He died on September 19, 1881.

But if it had not been for divine Providence, Garfield would never have lived his brief fifty years.

As a sixteen-year-old teenager, Garfield worked on a canal boat named *The Evening Star.* When he went on duty one midnight, it was raining as he took his turn at the bow. When he picked up a rope on deck and began to pull on it, the rope caught and wouldn't budge. He gave it another strong pull, and the rope freed itself and Garfield fell back into the dark waters.

As he plunged beneath the dark waters of the canal, Garfield clung to the rope. Suddenly, the slack was gone. Much to his relief, the rope became taut in his hand. Scared out of his wits, young Garfield quickly pulled himself back on deck.

Later, back on board the boat, he picked up the rope and threw it toward the crevice in which it had been caught the night before. Although he threw the rope scores of times, it never once caught in the crevice.

Concluding that God had saved his life for a purpose, young Garfield determined to make something of himself. Quitting his job on the canal, he went home to Ohio. When he walked into his home, he found his mother on her knees, praying for his safety.

This unknown psalmist learned the lesson centuries ago that his greatest help came from God. We do not know who this psalmist was or what personal problems he faced that made him reach out to God. But in these eight verses of Scripture, we read the testimony of a man who discovered God in the darkness. And now he testified from his own experience that there is help from on high for those who will claim it.

Look at four simple things this psalm teaches us:

I. The source of our help (vv. 1-2).
   1. It is from above.
   2. It is from the creator.
II. The strength of our help (v. 3).
   1. It is personal.
   2. It is vigilant.
III. The surety of our help (v. 4).
   1. It is tried and proved.
   2. It is always dependable.
IV. The scope of our help (vv. 5-8).
   1. It covers our physical needs (vv. 5-6).
   2. It covers our spiritual needs (v. 7).
   3. It covers time and eternity (v. 8).

Conclusion:

Dudley Dennison, Jr., in his book *Windows, Ladders and Bridges,* tells about a farmer who printed the words *God Is Love* on his weather vane. When someone asked the farmer if he meant that God is as fickle as the wind, the farmer replied: "No, I mean that God is love whichever way the wind blows."

"If the wind is from the cold north, God is love. If the wind is blowing out of the east, God is love. If the wind blows from the south, God is love. And if the wind blows out of the west, still God is love," the farmer said.

Help from on high is as dependable as the love of God.

23
Hold On Until Daylight

Scripture: Genesis 32:24-31

Introduction:

When my dad was a young man, he lost his wife. It was a terribly difficult experience because they had a small girl who was about three years old. My dad lost his wife, and she lost her mother.

In the dark hours of the night before she died, his wife turned to him and said, "Bud, I think I can make it if I can just hold on 'till daylight."

A lot of us have felt that way. Some cross has been so heavy that it has cast a dark shadow over our lives. With tear-filled eyes and heavy hearts we have walked on, hoping and praying for a better day. We have said to ourselves, "I think I can make it if I can just hold on 'til daylight."

That was exactly how Jacob felt. Twenty years before the events of this passage, Jacob had stolen the birthright from his twin brother Esau. Because of Jacob's deception, he had to leave home. Under the guise of sending Jacob off to find a wife, his mother, Rebecca, sent him to Haran.

Jacob prospered during those twenty years, but as he traveled on his way back home, word reached him that Esau and his men were coming out to meet him.

On the night before the two brothers met, Jacob got off to himself to think matters over. During the night, verse 24 states: "And Jacob was left alone; and there wrestled a man with him until the breaking of the day."

As we pass through our dark crisis, hoping and praying that things will get better, Jacob shows us three steps we can take:

I. We must do what we can (vv. 17-24).

1. Prepare others for what may come (vv. 22-23).
2. Prepare ourselves for what may come (vv. 13-21).
II. We must pray the matter through (vv. 9-12,24-26).
    1. Fear will drive us to our knees (vv. 9-12).
    2. We must claim God's promises (v. 12).
    3. We must pray it through alone (v. 24).
    4. We must hold on until the answer comes (vv. 24-29).
III. We must walk by faith (vv. 13-26,27-31).
    1. Other resources are inadequate (vv. 13-21).
    2. The light will come (v. 24).
    3. God will bless (vv. 25-31).

Conclusion:

Dr. Norman Vincent Peale, former pastor of Marble Collegiate Church in New York City, tells in his book *Stay Alive All Your Life* about encountering a hurricane in the Atlantic.

After the ship had safely skirted the outer edge of the storm, Dr. Peale and the captain were visiting. The captain said he had lived by the philosophy that if the sea is smooth, it will get rough, and if it is rough, it will get smooth. Then the captain added: "But with a good ship you can always ride it out."

Life will not always be smooth for us. When the way is trying and the darkness descends about us, what shall we do?

Jacob's example gives us the answer: hold on to God in prayer and faith until daylight comes.

24
Hurrying Toward Heaven

Scripture: *Revelation 7:13-17*

Introduction:

Soon, life will be over. Each of us who is a Christian is hurrying toward heaven. Time waits for none of us. For any of us, heaven may come at any moment.

When I was pastor in west Texas, my funny, wonderful friend

Emmy Lynn suddenly went to be with Jesus. One of those people who is a constant surprise and delight, she was well along in years.

She got up one Sunday morning and dressed in her best clothes. She intended to worship her Lord in her church, but she didn't. For on that Sunday, she went to church in heaven.

Mrs. Lynn wasn't feeling too well that Sunday morning, so on her way to church she went by to see the doctor. But while she waited to see the physician, the Great Physician came and took her to her heavenly home.

She didn't know it, but that morning as she dressed to go to church, she was hurrying toward heaven. And so it is with each of us who is a Christian.

I hear John saying this in the text we are considering. The Christians of Asia Minor, in the year AD 95, were suffering greatly under the pagan hand of Emperor Domitian. Persecution—even death—was the fate of many believers.

In his revelation, John saw these and other saints coming out of their great tribulation on earth into the blissful rest of the heavenly home. Some have already arrived. Some are still arriving. Even as John watched, he saw the persecuted, dying believers hurrying into heaven. They were arriving home.

As we consider the sobering fact that with every heartbeat we, too, are hurrying toward heaven, there are three things we must bear in mind:

  I. The preparation we must make (v. 14).
    1. It is personal.
    2. It is by the blood.
  II. The participation we shall share (v. 15).
    1. We shall be with the Heavenly Father.
    2. We shall serve the Heavenly Father.
    3. We shall fellowship with the saints.
  III. The provision we shall enjoy (vv. 16-17).
    1. All needs shall be met (v. 16).
    2. Jesus shall supply them (v. 17).

Conclusion:

Walter Knight tells about Zenophon and ten thousand of his men who were retreating. After suffering many hardships, they finally came to a hill, and in the distance they could see the blue waves of the Mediterranean. Suddenly, they broke into a shout: "The Sea! The Sea!"

All that separated them from their homes and loved ones was the sea. And they knew that with good fortune, they would soon be home.

25
Jewels from King Solomon's Mine

Scripture: 1 Kings 4:29-34

Introduction:

The largest diamond ever discovered was the Cullinan diamond. It was found in 1905 in the Premier Mine of South Africa. It weighed 3,106 carats or about one and one-third pounds. The second largest diamond ever found was the Jonker diamond. It was mined in 1934 and weighed 736 carats.

There are only three important diamond fields in the world today. They are located in India, South America, and Africa. Today, Africa produces about 97 percent of the world's supply of diamonds. Since these diamond mines were discovered in Africa in 1866, more than one billion dollars worth of diamonds have been mined from them.

But in this message we shall consider a mine and jewels of another type. The mine in which we shall dig is the Book of Proverbs. It is King Solomon's mine. And the jewels we shall find in this mine are worth keeping and treasuring.

Let me share with you three of the many jewels found in King Solomon's mine.

    I. A loving spirit (Prov. 10:12).
        1. What hate does.
        2. What love does.
    II. A happy disposition (Prov. 17:22).
        1. What happiness does.
        2. What depression does.

III. A humble attitude (Prov. 16:18-19).
   1. What pride does (v. 18).
   2. What humility does (v. 19).

Conclusion:
   Dr. George W. Truett told about a girl who was naturally happy, but when she became a Christian she was even happier.
   One day someone told the girl's straight-faced, straight-laced, sour-puss aunt that her niece was so beautifully radiant. The old aunt replied that apparently the work of God's grace was not yet complete in the niece's life because she seemed to be more addicted to laughter than ever before.
   There are some things to which Christians ought to be addicted, and laughter is certainly one of them. But add to this the three things mentioned here by the wisest man who ever lived: a loving spirit; a happy disposition; and a humble attitude.

26
Keeping Fit Spiritually

Scripture: *Joshua 23:6-13*

Introduction:
   More than any generation in history, our generation is acutely aware of the need for physical fitness. We know more about the importance and cultivation of good health than has ever been known.
   Television constantly warns us about the dangers of alcohol, tobacco, and other drugs. The spas and health clubs are doing a booming business, overrun with flabby folks. The golf courses are crowded with pudgy, middle-aged men and women, scooting across the green fairways in their little carts. And the roads are so crowded with joggers, bicyclists, and walkers that it's hardly safe to drive.
   We ought to keep fit physically, but in doing so we must not substitute the good for the best. What about keeping fit spiritu-

ally? Modern men and women are rightly concerned about their bodies, but what about their spirits? Little attention is given to the most important matters of life.

In this passage of Scripture, Joshua tells us how to keep fit spiritually. He was, as verse 1 declares, "old and stricken in age." He lived to be 110, and these are some of the last words Joshua ever spoke.

Under his leadership the Israelites had moved out of the wilderness, across the Jordan, and into the Promised Land. For years, now, they had lived and prospered in Canaan.

Realizing that death was near, one more time Joshua reminded the Jews of their blessings from God and their responsibilities to God. And in verses 6-13 he gave to them and to us the key to keeping fit spiritually.

I. Stay with the Word.
   1. Accept it (v. 6).
     "Do all that is written in the book of the law of Moses . . . turn not aside therefore;"
   2. Absorb it (v. 6).
     "Keep and do all."

II. Stay from the world.
   1. Guard your affections (v. 7).
     "Come not among these nations, . . . neither make mention of their gods."
   2. To fail to do so will bring afflictions (v. 13).
     "They shall be snares and traps unto you and scourges in your sides, and thorns in your eyes, until you perish from off this good land."

III. Stay in the Lord.
   1. Make an open acknowledgment of Him (v. 8).
     "But cleave unto the Lord your God."
     "Take good heed therefore unto yourselves, that ye love the Lord your God" (v. 11).
   2. Cultivate a strong attachment to Him (v. 8).
     "But cleave unto the Lord your God, as ye have done unto this day."

Conclusion:

In their book *Success Through a Positive Mental Attitude*, Napoleon Hill and Clement Stone say that summoning courage to take the first step in any endeavor is the most important thing a person can do to accomplish his goal.

They relate the story of a sixty-three-year-old grandmother, Mrs. Charles Philipia, who decided she was going to walk from New York City to Miami, Florida. When she finally reached Miami, she was interviewed by a newspaperman who wanted to know if making such a long journey on foot hadn't frightened her.

"How did you ever summon courage to do it?" he asked.

Mrs. Philipia replied: "It doesn't take courage to take one step and that's all I did really. I just took one step. And then I took another step. And then another and another and here I am."

Joshua shows us here that keeping fit spiritually is a matter of taking one spiritual step at a time: we must stay with the Word, stay away from the world, and stay in the Lord.

27
Life's Dark Gethsemanes

Scripture: *James 1:1-8 (NASB)*

Introduction:

Arthur John Gossip was an outstanding Scottish preacher who died in 1954. When he was pastor of the Beechgrove Church in Aberdeen, Scotland, his wife died. The year was 1927.

On the first Sunday after he had buried his wife, Dr. Gossip preached in his church as usual. And the message he brought that morning, "But When Life Tumbles In, What Then?" was probably the best sermon he ever preached.

Sustained by his strong faith, the lonely, heartbroken pastor told his people: "I don't think you need to be afraid of life. Our hearts are very frail; and there are places where the road is very steep and very lonely. But we have a wonderful God."[1]

Referring to Hopeful, a character in Bunyan's *The Pilgrim's*

Progress, Gossip said that as Hopeful entered the chilling waters of death he called back to those behind him: "Be of good cheer, my brother. I feel the bottom and it is good."

Sooner or later each of us will face life's dark Gethsemanes. As an old Arabic proverb puts it, "Sooner or later the black camel kneels in front of every tent."

When life's dark Gethsemanes overtake us, and we are forced to walk that lonely road, what shall we do and how shall we respond?

James has something to say about life's dark Gethsemanes and how the believer should face them.

I. They will come to all of us.
    1.   They are certain (v. 2).
       "When you encounter various trials."
    2.   God's people are not immune (v. 2).
       "My brethren."
    3.   They may be numerous (v. 2).
       "When you encounter various trials."

II. They must be faced in the right spirit.
    1.   Choose your response before it's needed (v. 2).
       "Count it." The way the word is written in the Greek, according to A. T. Robertson, it means "do it now and once for all."
    2.   Choose to respond positively (v. 2).
       "Consider it all joy" (NASB). Robertson says, "whole joy," "unmixed joy," "not just 'some joy' along with much grief."
    3.   God will show us how to respond (vv. 5-8).
       Robertson says: "To have a shortage of wisdom (not just knowledge . . . but wisdom . . . the practical use of knowledge)." But we are to "keep on asking" (v. 5).

III. They will bring good to us.
    1.   Experience teaches us this (v. 3).
       "Knowing this. . . ." The word "know" indicates experiential knowledge.
    2.   The Bible teaches us this (vv. 3-4).
       "Knowing that the testing of your faith produces endurance. And let endurance have its perfect result, that you may be perfect and complete, lacking in nothing" (NASB). (See also Rom. 8:28.)

Conclusion:

The wife of a young professor who taught in the seminary from which I was graduated died suddenly. She had undergone surgery and was making a good recovery and was sent home. Suddenly, she became ill and was rushed back to the hospital and in a matter of only a few hours, she died.

I was on the seminary campus not long after the professor's wife died. Some of his friends, other professors in the seminary, told me that in a recent chapel service their sorrowing professor friend gave a marvelous testimony to the sustaining grace of the Lord Jesus Christ and how He is able to meet all of our needs.

It's true. Jesus is both able and willing to sustain us as we walk through life's dark Gethsemanes.

---

1. From *20 Centuries of Great Preaching* by Clyde Fant and Bill Pinson, vol. VIII, pp. 227-228, copyright © 1971; used by permission of Word Books, Publisher, Waco, Texas 76796.

28
Live and Like It

Scripture: Numbers 21:11

Introduction:

The Menninger Clinic of Topeka, Kansas, is known around the world. It is one of the best-known psychiatric clinics in America.

Dr. Karl Menninger, a respected psychiatrist, says that "most Americans today exist without purpose and without significance."

I believe he is saying that millions of Americans aren't enjoying life. What a tragedy this is because we are stuck with it. It is the only one we have. We ought to enjoy it.

The passage which we are using for this text appeals both to my spirit and imagination. It contains, for me at least, an encouragement to enjoy life as I live it.

Using some sanctified imagination, let me divide this text into three statements and comment briefly on each of them.

    I. The trip before us (v. 11).
        "And they journeyed."
        1. Life is a journey.
        2. Life is a journey we must make.
   II. The trials about us (v. 11).
        "In the wilderness."
        1. It is often a difficult journey.
        2. We can learn from our difficulties.
  III. The temperament within us (v. 11).
        "Toward the sunrising."
        1. We must live in hope.
        2. We must look toward tomorrow.

Conclusion:

When American architect Frank Lloyd Wright was eighty-three years old, someone asked him which of his works he would say was his best one. And quickly Wright replied, "My next one."

That's the "Wright" attitude. That's what I would call journeying toward the sunrise. A person who faces life with that kind of temperament will never be defeated.

It was said of Ian Maclaren, the great Scottish preacher, that he had a great eye for the sunrise.

What an epitaph! What a way to face life. It is a foolproof philosophy for making sure that we face life optimistically and like it as we live it.

29
Love that Lasts

Scripture: *Ephesians 5:22-2£*

Introduction:

In his book *Illustrations for Preaching,* Benjamin P. Browne tells about an old sea captain and Trumbie's Reef, along the coast of Maine.

The old captain went to sea when he was only a boy and sailed around the world, finally becoming captain of his own ship.

Stormy voyages and dangerous harbors were no stranger to the old captain. In his frequent voyages, he had often encountered many dangers, but he had always managed to guide his ship through the fiercest storm or into the most treacherous harbor. He was a skilled sailor, and he had great confidence in his own ability.

At the end of his long and enviable career, he sailed back to his home port in Maine, a place where he was perfectly at ease because he knew every rock and reef.

But when he sailed his ship into the Maine harbor where he had sailed as a boy, and which he knew like the back of his hand, his ship was wrecked on Trumbie's Reef. Though he had sailed the seven seas, he piled up on the rocks near home.

There is a lesson in this story for each of us. Home is the place where we let down our defenses and relax. But if love is to last, and if the home is to endure, then we must beware of the rocks nearest home.

Paul tells us how to make love last. Here are three suggestions to consider.

    I. For love to last it must be unselfish.

        1. The wife's attitude.

"Wives, submit yourselves unto your own husbands, as unto the Lord" (v. 22).

The one duty of the wife upon which Paul insists in this passage is that of submission. It is a duty placed on her by the Savior. Though the wife stands on an equal footing in Christ with her husband, this is the special role given to her. The wife's unselfish love inspires her to submit herself to her husband's leadership. His unselfish love inspires him always to seek her best.

    2.   The husband's attitude.

"Husbands, love your wives, even as Christ also loved the church, and gave himself for it" (v. 25). The word for *love* is from the same word used in John 3:16: love that sacrifices itself for the welfare of the beloved. It is the kind of love Christ has for the church. This kind of love carefully protects the submissive wife. If need be, the husband will die for his wife.

II. For love to last it must be caring.

    1.   It is so caring that it forgets self (v. 22).

"Wives, submit yourselves. . . . Husbands, love your wives" (vv. 22,25).

    2.   It is so caring that it is sacrificial.

"Wives, . . . husbands, love . . . as Christ also loved the church, and gave himself for it" (vv. 22,25).

    3.   It is so caring that it brings out the best in each of them (vv. 26-28).

III. For love to last it must be well founded.

epitaph on an old New England headstone: "Here lies the body of Obidiah Wilkinson and Ruth, his wife, their warfare is accomplished."

But a love that rests on the right kind of foundation will have some peace and contentment.

    1.   It is built on the fear of God.

"Submitting yourselves one to another in the fear of God" (v. 21).

    2.   It is built on mutual respect.

"Wives, submit yourselves unto your own husbands. . . . Husbands, love your wives" (vv. 22,25).

    3.   It is built on a mutual love for Christ (vv. 24-25).

Conclusion:

The parents of renowned missionary David Livingstone are buried in Blantyre, Scotland, not far from Glasgow.

On their headstone one can read these words: "To show the resting place of Neil Livingstone and Agnes Hunter, his wife, and to express the thankfulness to God of their children, John, David, Janet, Charles, and Agnes, for poor and pious parents."

"Poor and pious parents," it reads. For love to last poverty is not necessary, but piety is.

Without a pious foundation—the fear of God and a mutual love for Christ—love will have a tough time lasting in this kind of world.

30
Making the Most of Life

Scripture: *Philippians 3:13-15*

Introduction:

Life would be a monotonous thing if it didn't threaten us with difficulties and challenge us with opportunities. We only make the most of life when we master our difficulties and respond to our opportunities.

When Sir Earnest Shackleton was preparing for one of his explorations to the South Pole, he wanted a crew on whom he could depend. The kind of men he wanted had to be men who had been tested and made strong by life's difficulties and challenges.

About the turn of the century he placed the following advertisement in a London newspaper: "Men wanted for hazardous journey, small wages, bitter cold, long months of complete darkness, constant danger, safe return doubtful. Honor and recognition in case of success."

Would any sane human respond to such challenge? Yes, thousands responded and begged to be given the privilege to risk all on the great venture.

In this passage of Scripture, Paul throws out to us life's greatest challenge: to make the most of life. And he points out in this text that to do it we must take at least these three steps:

I. We must forget some things in the past (v. 13).
   1. We must forget past sins and failures.
      When God forgives our sins, He forgets them. We ought to seek His forgiveness and then forget our sins.
   2. We must forget our past sorrows and successes.
      Both sorrow and success, treasured and clutched to our bosoms, will hold us back and hinder our progress.
II. We must be dissatisfied with some things in the present.
   1. We must be dissatisfied with ourselves.
      We should never dislike ourselves, but we should never be satisfied with self as it is. Within each believer there must be the holy urge to improve.
   2. We must be dissatisfied with ourselves in the light of our possibilities.
      Within us there are giants that need to be awakened, and we must not be satisfied to live midget-kind of lives.
III. We must struggle towards some things in the future (v. 14).
      Life is measured in three dimensions: past, present, and future. The past is gone and cannot be changed. The future lies before us and it can be changed.
   1. God gave us a "holy reach" toward the future. "I . . . reach forth" (v. 13).
   2. We must believe the future will be better than the past.
      Although the future is a mystery, it is a glorious open door through which we can walk to greater accomplishments.

Conclusion:

Faith, hope, prayer, and hard work will help us make the most of life. It is no secret why some have succeeded so magnificently.

Michelangelo, it is told, often slept with his clothes on, so he could get back to his work without losing time in dressing. Is there any wonder then that he succeeded so brilliantly?

Sir Walter Scott, bankrupt and goaded on by the desire to clear his name of any blemish, wrote the "Waverly Novels" at the rate of one every thirty days. Is it any wonder then that he succeeded so brilliantly?

Almost without exception, men and women in every type of pursuit have won success at the cost of dedication, faith, and prodigious work.

31
Man in Conference With God

Scripture: *Isaiah 1:1-20*

Introduction:

A small boy had disobeyed his mother, and she had been forced to correct him. Pouting and angry because his mother had punished him, the boy decided he would hide and not answer when she called him. He wanted her to think something terrible had happened to him.

It wasn't long before the mother missed her son and began a frantic search for him. After a rather long and frightening search, she found him in his hiding place. Picking him up and holding him close to her heart, she sobbed, "Why didn't you come when I called you? You have made Mother very sad. We could have worked this thing out together."

That's the message of God to Judah through Isaiah, His prophet. God's grief over Judah's rebellion is summed up in verse 18: "Come now, and let us reason together, saith the Lord: though your sins be as scarlet, they shall be as white as snow: though they be red like crimson, they shall be as wool."

God was saying to ancient Judah, and to us through His Holy Spirit, "Bring your sins to Me. We can work things out together."

The late Dr. R. G. Lee had a sermon on this text titled: "Man in Conference with God." Since I cannot improve on it, I borrow his title with gratitude.

I. An Indictment (vv. 4-6).
  1. Guilty of rebelling against God (v. 4).
  2. Guilty of forsaking God (v. 4).
  3. Guilty of despising God (v. 4).
  4. Guilty of total corruption (vv. 5-6).
II. A Pardon.
  1. It is available (v. 18).
  2. It does not come through man's sacrifices (vv. 12-15).
  3. It comes from God (v. 18).
  4. It is powerful (v. 18).
III. A Promise.
  1. To those who respond to the invitation (v. 19).
  2. To those who refuse to respond to the invitation (v. 19).

Conclusion:

In New York State there is a cemetery in which there is a strange headstone. There is no name on it. There are no dates. The stone has no sculptor's etchings on it. And there is no epitaph.

On the strange headstone in the New York cemetery there is cut only one word: "Forgiven."

That's what God offered to rebellious Judah, and that's what He offers to sinful, rebellious mankind in our day. God freely offers to us the thing we most need.

32
Man's Greatest Need

Scripture: Ephesians 2:1-10

Introduction:
What is mankind's greatest need? Is it for food, clothing, shelter, or health?

No, it is none of these, although each is important.

During World War II, Captain Eddie Rickenbacker's airplane crashed at sea. For twenty-one days Rickenbacker and his crew were lost in the Pacific. And the world despaired for their lives. Finally, through a series of miracles, Rickenbacker and his men were rescued.

When Rickenbacker returned to the United States, he toured veteran's hospitals and spoke to large groups of servicemen. Rickenbacker's constant message to them was: "Men, if you have not had an experience of God in your life, my advice is to get busy and get yourself one."

That's man's greatest need. Nothing is more important. Receiving Jesus Christ as our personal Savior must be our first priority.

Paul discussed man's greatest need in this passage of Scripture.

    I. The need for salvation (vv. 1-3).
       1. Spiritually dead (v. 1).
       2. Controlled by Satan (v. 2).
       3. Objects of God's wrath (v. 3).
    II. The provision of salvation (vv. 4-5).
       1. Provided by God (v. 4).
       2. Provided through God's mercy and love (v. 4).
       3. Provided when we most needed it (v. 5).
   III. The power of salvation (vv. 5-6).

1. Through it we are made alive (v. 5).
2. Through it we have fellowship with Christ (v. 6).
IV. The purpose of salvation (v. 7).
   1. Demonstrates God's rich grace (v. 7).
   2. Glorifies Jesus Christ (v. 7).
V. The plan of salvation (vv. 8-10).
   1. Operates by grace (v. 8).
   2. Appropriated by faith (v. 8).
   3. Is apart from works (vv. 8-9).
   4. Is solely through Christ (v. 10).
   5. Produces good works (v. 10).

Conclusion:

George W. Truett, in his book *Sermons from Paul*, related that Sir James Simpson, who discovered the anesthetic properties of chloroform, was once asked what he considered his greatest discovery.

The great Edinburgh physician answered: "The greatest discovery I have ever made is that Jesus Christ has saved me, a poor sinner."

33
Measuring the Greatness of God

Scripture: Deuteronomy 33:26-29

Introduction:

American astronomer Dr. Harlow Shapley, a former professor of astronomy at Harvard University, said there may be as many as 100 million other planets which are suitable for higher forms of life.

No one knows for sure whether Shapley's statement is true, but this fact is undeniable: the universe and the solar system point undeniably to the greatness of God.

The sun is 865,370 miles in diameter, but the moon is only

2,160 miles in diameter. The earth, which is only 7,926 miles in diameter, is so small that it would take a million earths to fill the interior of the sun.

While earthlings still wrangle over the safety of nuclear energy, it is the burning of nuclear fuel that causes the sun to burn with a surface temperature of 10,000° Farenheit.

Every 365 days, the sun uses up about 22 quadrillion tons of hydrogen in producing its energy. And authorities say that it still contains enough hydrogen to shine for another five billion years before its light will begin to fade.

According to Dr. Shapely, the Milky Way, to which our solar system belongs, is 300,000 light years wide. This means that a traveler traveling across it at the speed of light, 186,282 miles per second, would have to travel twenty-four hours a day, 365 days a year, for 300,000 years before getting across it.

In our own galaxy, there are something like 100 billion stars. But we can see only about 6,000 of these stars from the earth with the naked eye.[1]

Moses, 120 years old and about to die, was contemplating the greatness of God when he said, in verse 26: "There is none like unto the God of Jeshurun."

Forbidden to enter Canaan, Moses delivered this farewell address, climbed Mount Nebo, looked over into the Promised Land, and died. But Moses looked back over a life of having walked with God and measured the greatness of God.

In measuring the greatness of God, Moses described for us:
  I. His great power (v. 26).
     1. He protects us.
     2. He guides us.
 II. His great compassion (v. 27).
     1. He dwells with us.
     2. He sustains us.
III. His great provision (vv. 28-29).
     1. He provides abundantly (v. 28).
     2. He provides graciously (v. 29).

Conclusion:

Many years ago, when I was a student in college, I learned a little poem that says a great deal about the greatness of God.

Thou art coming to a king,
With thee great petitions bring,
For His grace and power are such,
None can ever ask too much.

AUTHOR UNKNOWN

34
Needed but Not Deserved

Scripture: Titus 2:11-14

Introduction:

Roy Angell relates that before S. M. Lindsay became a pastor in America, he taught a class of boys in a Sunday School in Scotland.

One day, according to Lindsay, he was walking down an icy street to attend an afternoon tea. He was dressed in a high top hat, striped trousers, a cutaway coat, and spats.

As he walked along the icy street, he saw Bobby, one of his Sunday School boys, lurking behind one of the bushes lining the street. Suddenly, without warning, an ice ball hit Lindsay on the side of the head, knocking his silk hat into the mud and causing Lindsay to see stars. He knew young Bobby was the culprit.

He went on to the tea wondering how he should respond to Bobby's mischief. And he decided that he would return good for evil.

Remembering that he had loaned his three-part fishing pole to Bobby a few days earlier, Lindsay went to the hardware store and bought another pole. Taking it to Bobby's house, he knocked at the door and asked if Bobby were home.

"Yes," Bobby's mother replied as she called Bobby. But Bobby didn't respond. He had gone out the back door when he saw his Sunday School teacher walking up to the front door.

Lindsay told Bobby's mother to give him the fishing pole and to tell him that his Sunday School teacher wanted him to have it. And he added, "Tell him I know he needs it."

A couple of hours later there was a timid knock at Lindsay's door. Opening the door, Lindsay saw Bobby sheepishly standing there with the fishing pole in hand.

"Mr. Lindsay," Bobby said quietly, "I'm returning your fishing pole. I need it, but I don't deserve it."

"Bobby," Mr. Lindsay said, "what was our Sunday School lesson about last Sunday?"

"Oh, Mr. Lindsay," Bobby replied, "I don't remember."

"Sure you do, Bobby. Don't you remember that it was a lesson about God's grace. And what did I tell you about God's grace?"

Bobby's eyes lightened up as he answered, "Oh, I remember now. You told us that grace is something we need but don't deserve."

There is no better definition of grace to be found anywhere. Grace, indeed, is something we need but don't deserve. We call it God's undeserved favor.

In this text, Paul talks to us about the grace of God which we need but don't deserve.

I. The availability of it.
   1. It is available to everyone (v. 11).
      "Hath appeared to all men."
      It is a reference to a specific happening in history: the birth of Jesus Christ in Nazareth. In Christ, grace and all its fullness came into the world. And it is available to all.
   2. It is available only in Christ (v. 14).
      "Who gave himself for us, that he might redeem us from all iniquity." Christ offered Himself for us to bring us the grace of God. It was a voluntary act on His part.
II. The demands of it.
      There is an instructional side to grace. It teaches us what God demands of us who receive His grace.
   1. Grace demands a new object of worship (v. 12).
      "Denying ungodliness."
   2. Grace demands a new set of morals (v. 12).
      "Denying . . . worldly lusts."
   3. Grace demands new attitudes (v. 12).
      "We should live soberly, righteously, and godly."

4. Grace demands immediate changes (v. 12).
"In this present world."
III. The hope of it.
Hope in the New Testament speaks of certainty and assurance. It is not a maybe-so thing as is our English word for *hope*.
1. In this present world (v. 12,14).
God's grace at work in our lives brings redemption, purity of life, and a new motive for right living.
2. In the world to come (v. 13).
Grace at work in our lives lifts our hopes beyond this life to the world to come. It points us away to the glorious day when Jesus shall come to receive us and take us home to live with Him.

Conclusion:

John Bunyan, author of *The Pilgrim's Progress,* once received notice that he had been drafted to serve in the English army. England was divided by civil war, and Bunyan was to fight in the siege of Leicester.

But as Bunyan was preparing to leave for the battle, a young man stepped up to take Bunyan's place. And in the battle that followed, the young man was shot through the head.

John Bunyan's life was saved by a substitute who died in his place.

Jesus Christ is our substitute. He died for us, bringing God's grace to us which we need but could never deserve.

35
Rescuing a Brother

Scripture: James 5:19-20

Introduction:

Carr P. Collins, late Baptist layman from Dallas who was president of Fidelity Union Life Insurance, wrote an article for "Lenten Guideposts" several years ago that was very moving.

The story was about Randy McKinley, a three-year-old boy, who was visiting his grandparents in south Texas. Suddenly, and without warning, the boy fell into a sixteen-inch pipe and plunged sixty-nine feet down a well.

Working nearby was a Mexican national named Manuel Corral. Although Corral's shoulders were one inch wider than the tubing of the well, he tied a rope to his feet, and three other braceros held him as he squirmed head first into the opening and descended into the blackness.

Finally, after what seemed an eternity, Corral's friends pulled him and Randy to safety. Corral's skin was cut and bleeding. His clothes had almost been shredded from his body. His shoulders were dislocated and his feet were so swollen he couldn't stand. But Corral rescued Randy, and the area proclaimed him a hero.

Each of us who is a Christian is to be a rescuer. James tells us in verses 19 and 20 that we are to be rescuers of our brothers when they "err from the truth."

Look at three things about rescuing a brother that are emphasized in this passage.

   I. The one to be rescued (v. 19).
      1. A Christian brother.
      2. An erring brother.
  II. The means of the rescue (v. 19).

1. Another believer's influence.
2. Another believer's compassion.
III. The results of the rescue (v. 20).
   1. Brings one back from sin.
   2. Saves one from death.

Conclusion:

American writer and poet James Russell Lowell once said he would be satisfied with this epitaph: "Here lies that part of James Russell Lowell which hindered him from doing well."

Although a believer has been given the divine nature, he still has the sinful nature with which to contend. Christians are going to sin, and when they do, other Christians must work in compassion and love to restore them.

36
Rules for a Happy Day

Scripture: *Psalm 118:24*

Introduction:

What is the one thing everybody wants? Why, it's happiness.

One eminent authority says that four out of five people are not as happy as they can be. And another states that unhappiness is the most common state of mind.

But what is happiness? Snoopy, Charlie Brown, Linus, and Lucy tell us what they think it is. They say that happiness is a thumb and a blanket; a warm puppy; an *A* on a spelling test; and finding someone you like at the front door.

They add that happiness is sleeping in your own bed; climbing a tree; being able to reach the doorknob; and knowing all the answers.

But genuine happiness is a state of contentment—peace of mind—and a sense of well-being. Happiness is that inner condition that causes one to be glad one is alive.

Countless books and millions of words have been written on

the subject of happiness. One psychologist says there are seven reasons for unhappiness: guilt, envy, irreligiousness, selfishness, self-pity, timidity, and worry. And a sociologist writes that there are only five things necessary for happiness: youth, money, success, good health, and a wife.

But a lot of people have all these qualities and are still miserable inside. The sociologist's five steps to happiness are too shallow.

There is no such thing as instant happiness. You can't store it up in the deep freeze and pull out enough of it to last through the week. Happiness is a thing that must be acquired day by day. It is a one-day-at-a-time process.

Let me suggest four simple rules for a happy day.

I. Accept today as a special gift (Ps. 118:24).
   1. It is from God.
   2. It is to be enjoyed.
II. Live today in gentle judgment of others (Matt. 7:1-5).
   1. It will come back to you (vv. 1-2).
   2. We all are sinners (vv. 3-5).
III. Don't measure yourself by others (Prov. 14:30;27:4).
   1. Envy destroys (Prov. 14:30).
   2. Jealousy defeats (Prov. 27:4).
IV. Start each day with God (Job 22:21; Ps. 55:17).
   1. Get to know Him (Job 22:21).
   2. Talk to Him daily (Ps. 55:17).

Conclusion:

In the 1975 edition of *The People's Almanac*, I read about some strange insurance policies carried by Lloyd's of London. One of their policies was called a "Happiness Policy," and it insured against a certain model developing worry lines on her face.

I don't know who the model was or if she ever had much of a problem with worry lines. But I know there is no such thing as a happiness policy which will guarantee that one will be happy when one pays the premiums.

But there are some positive steps we can take day by day—some rules we can follow—that will point us in the direction of living a happy life.

37
Secret Sins

Scripture: Joshua 7:1

Introduction:

In Nathaniel Hawthorne's *Mosses from an Old Manse,* a chapter titled "A Virtuoso's Collection" describes a mythical visit Hawthorne made to an imaginary museum. One day, with nothing better to do, he bought a fifty-cent ticket and went to see the things collected in the museum. Inside, he met a middle-aged man called the Virtuoso.

The Virtuoso showed Hawthorne many interesting things: a room filled with stuffed animals, including the wolf that had eaten Little Red Riding Hood; the old she wolf that had suckled Romulus and Remus; a white horse with the black head of an ox; Bucephalus, the mighty war horse of Alexander the Great; and Argus, the faithful dog of Ulysses.

They next went into an alcove filled with stuffed birds perched on tree branches. And there Hawthorne saw the white dove that Noah had sent from the ark, with a branch of withered olive leaves in her mouth.

Wandering through the museum, Hawthorne was shown Excalibur, the sword of King Arthur, and the sword of Brutus, long ago rusted by the blood of Julius Caeser. Nearby was the lance of Don Quixote and the shield of Achilles.

As Hawthorne continued his imaginary journey through the museum, he was shown a big bundle that was wrapped in sackcloth. The bundle was tightly tied with cords and the Virtuoso told Hawthorne, "It is the Christian's burden of sin."

"Oh, pray let us open it," Hawthorne begged. "For many a year I have longed to know its contents."

The Virtuoso refused. "Look into your own consciousness

and memory," he replied. "You will find there a list of whatever it contains."

Like Hawthorne, you and I know what's in that bundle. No one needs to open that hideous bag and parade the Christian's secret sins before us. We know them, for we have lived with them all too long. We recognize their ugly faces and know their awful power.

Long ago Achan learned about secret sins. Before Israel marched against Jericho, the people were told to seize the city's wealth and put it in the divine treasury.

But Achan had his own plans. He disobeyed the divine commandment, took some of the silver and gold and some of the beautiful clothing for himself, and hid them in his tent.

Achan was put on trial and convicted. When he was found guilty, he and his whole family were stoned to death in the valley of Achor. Then, they were cremated.

Achan's sad biography of secret sins speaks to our own hearts about our secret sins that need to be confessed and forsaken.

   I. The nature of them.
- 1. They are against God (Josh. 6:18-19; 7:20).
- 2. They are against ourselves (Josh. 7:1,16-26).
- 3. They are against others (Josh. 7:1-5,24-25).

  II. The progressiveness of them.
- 1. First the thought (Josh. 7:21).
  "I saw."
- 2. Then the desire (Josh. 7:21).
  "Then I coveted them."
- 3. Then the act (Josh. 7:21).
  "And [I] took them."

 III. The consequences of them.
- 1. They bring shame (Josh. 7:20).
- 2. They bring disgrace (Josh. 7:23).
- 3. They bring judgment (Josh. 7:24-26).

 IV. The response to them.
- 1. Confession to God (Josh. 7:19-20).
- 2. Confession to those wronged (Josh. 7:19).

Conclusion:

In his book *Let Me Illustrate*, Donald Grey Barnhouse tells about a sign that once hung above a piece of complicated machinery in a textile factory. The sign read, "If your threads get tangled, call the foreman."

One day a woman was busily working and got her threads tangled. When she tried to disentangle them, she only made matters worse. Finally, in desperation, she called the foreman. Looking at the mess the woman had made, the foreman asked, "Why didn't you call for me like the sign says?"

"Well," responded the woman, "I thought I could untangle them myself."

"But the sign instructed you to call for me," the foreman said sternly.

"But," she replied, "I did my best."

And the foreman quickly answered, "Your best is not good enough. The next time you have a problem like this, call for me."

Have you been trying to do it yourself—trying to handle your secret sins and untangle your life in your own strength? Well, friend, that's not good enough. It won't work.

The only way to handle secret sins is to call for the divine Foreman. Jesus Christ specializes in untangling the threads of life that we have knotted.

Send for Him! Make a confession of that secret sin to Him. Only He can help untangle the knots of life that secret sins have tied.

38
Strength to Hold On

Scripture: Isaiah 40:28-31

Introduction:

John A. Redhead, in his book *Living All Your Life,* relates a story from the pen of Lloyd Lewis that pretty well describes twentieth-century life.

In the battle of Shiloh, Lewis related, the Union army was

pushed back by General Albert Sydney Johnston and his Confederate army.

The retreating Yankee troops came to a river, and some of their artillery bogged down in the mud of the riverbank. One teamster was pushing hard on a stuck gun carriage when an evangelist with the troops chose an inopportune time to bear a witness.

"Do you know who died on the cross?" the evangelist asked the muddy, weary soldier. And without even raising his head, the exasperated Yankee trooper replied, "Don't ask me any riddles! I'm stuck in the mud."

This is the pitiful cry of all humanity. Only the person who is blind fails to see that all men and women everywhere are having a hard time of it in one way or another. In some way, each of us is stuck in the mud.

This passage from Isaiah addresses this very thing. Here the people of Judah are pictured in Exile in Babylon. They are distressed, away from their beloved Jerusalem, separated from their holy Temple, and about ready to give up.

In their darkest hour, wondering how in the world they could hold on to their faith and hope, God had a word for them.

Needing strength to hold on, God promised it to them in this great passage.

I. The need for this strength.

Disease devastates us. Problems plague us. Sorrows subdue us. Trials tear at us. What we need is strength just to hold on.

The father of Alexander the Great was Philip of Macedon, for whom the ancient city of Philippi was named. Philip appointed a servant to stand daily in the king's presence and whisper in his ear, "Philip, remember thou art mortal!"

You and I know we are mortal. Our weaknesses continually remind us of this. Daily, we are reminded how great is our need for spiritual strength.

1. Because life's trials exhaust us.

"To the faint . . . to them that have no might . . . faint and be weary . . . men . . . utterly fall" (vv. 29-30).

2. Because it is our only hope.

All other resources had failed Judah. She was powerless in the face of her problems: youths fainted, and the young men fell; God alone could help (v. 30).

II. The availability of this strength.

A Fort Worth, Texas, paper carried a sad story on August 8, 1972. It told about the suicide of Professor Robert William Jung, a former professor at Southern Methodist University in Dallas, who was regarded as an expert on suicide. But this expert on the prevention of suicide didn't find the strength to hold on when his crisis was the greatest. But that strength is available.

1. This strength is available in our God.

"The everlasting God, the Lord, the Creator of the ends of the earth, fainteth not, neither is weary" (v. 28).

2. This strength is available without charge.

"He giveth power to the faint" (v. 29). Notice the word *giveth*.

3. This strength is available to everyone who needs it.

"Even the youths shall faint and be weary, and the young men shall utterly fall: But they that wait upon the Lord shall renew their strength" (vv. 30-31).

4. This strength is available by faith.

"But they that wait upon the Lord shall renew their strength" (v. 31). Notice the word *wait*.

III. The sufficiency of this strength.

I read sometime ago that in one bolt of lightning that flashes out of a thunderstorm, there is enough electricity dissipated to light every light bulb and turn every electric motor in the city of Dallas for one month. And I have also read that in the average hurricane, there is expended in one hour enough electricity to supply all the power the United States needs for a full year. God's strength is sufficient for our greatest problem.

1. This strength is sufficient for the weakest among us.

"He giveth power to the faint; and to them that have no might" (v. 29).

2. This strength is sufficient for our most difficult trial.

"They shall mount up with wings as eagles; they shall run, and not be weary; and they shall walk and not faint" (v. 31).

Conclusion:

A Swiss expedition set out to climb Mount Everest several years ago. According to their leader, the earth's highest mountain is still growing. It used to be 29,002 feet high, but now it is 29,610 feet above sea level. As the earth's crust continues to buckle, the mountain continues to get higher.

Do you sometimes feel that way about life? Is life getting tougher and more difficult for you every day? Do you feel your strength is totally inadequate to face life's huge problems?

Take hope! Strength to conquer is available through our blessed Lord so that "they that wait upon the Lord shall renew their strength; they shall mount up with wings as eagles; they shall run, and not be weary; and they shall walk, and not faint" (v. 31).

39
Sweet Glimpses into Glory

Scripture: Revelation 21:1-5

Introduction:

When I was pastor in Lubbock, Texas, my black pastor friend, Dr. Lawton, died. The black minister who held Lawton's funeral service was a capable preacher, and he told the following story.

"When I was a boy living in east Texas," he said, "I lived with my grandparents.

"We had a good many hogs which we called 'house hogs.' They were called this because they stayed near the house most of the time.

"Occasionally, these 'house hogs' would wander down to the bottomland where they grazed on the acorns," he continued.

"Grandfather never wanted them to be gone too long at a time, for fear they would wander off and not return."

The preacher continued his story. By this time, he had my complete, almost-breathless attention.

"Grandfather would pick up a basket, go by the corncrib, fill it with corn, and walk toward the distant bottomland," he said.

"When he found the hogs, he wouldn't throw out the entire basket of corn at one time. Rather, walking back toward the house and shelling the corn as he walked, he would throw a little corn on the ground, calling the hogs at the same time. Before long, Grandfather had all the hogs back at the house where they belonged," he concluded.

Then the minister made his point: "Jesus does us about the same way," he said. "We don't know very much about heaven, but now and then, He throws out to us a verse—a picture of what it's like. He tells us just a little bit about heaven, here and there in the Bible, and as we follow Him step by step and day by day, we finally reach our heavenly home."

In Revelation 21 and 22, Jesus gave John some sweet glimpses into glory. He showed John that:

   I. Heaven is a place of perfect fellowship (v. 3; 22:4).
     1. With the Father.
     2. With the redeemed.
  II. Heaven is a place of perfect protection (vv. 4, 12-14).
     1. From sorrow (v. 4).
     2. From pain (v. 4).
     3. From all that would harm (vv. 12-14).
 III. Heaven is a place of perfect provision (22:1-2).
     1. Sufficient provision (vv. 1-2).
     2. Abundant provision (v. 2).

Conclusion:

When I was a young pastor and still in the seminary, an old saint told me about a vision she had. She and her husband were godly people, and I clung to her every word.

They had lost a grown son some months before I became pastor of the church, and the dear old mother was broken-hearted. One day as she lay down in the afternoon to rest, she told me, she saw a vision of her son. She was wide awake, and suddenly there appeared to her in her room a bright light, and the face of her son appeared in that light.

"Mother," he said, "don't be anxious and fretful anymore. It is so wonderful and beautiful over here."

The old mother then told me that from that time on she had peace in her heart about her son.

40
Tempted to Quit

Scripture: *Hebrews 10:32-39*

Introduction:

My Methodist friend Dr. Gaston Foote, pastor emeritus of First Methodist Church, Fort Worth, Texas, tells how proud he was the first day his dad let him go to the field to plow with his older brothers.

Foote had just finished the eighth grade, and he felt he was old enough to handle a plow. He kept nagging his dad about it until his father rigged up a plow and an old mule and sent young Gaston to the field to work with his brothers.

The old mule was so gentle that he could do the plowing without the boy, but Foote swelled with pride as the old mule dragged him up and down the rows.

Shortly after lunch, the sand of the field was so hot young Foote's bare feet almost blistered, but he couldn't afford to complain. About the middle of the afternoon, the hot, broiling sun had taken its toll, and the boy was so bone tired that he tied the lines around his waist and let the tough-mouthed old mule do the rest.

But when Foote stopped plowing, his father looked at the sun and told him there was still time to do plenty of plowing. And it was there, under the hot summer sun, that young Foote learned an unforgettable lesson.

Putting his hand on his son's shoulder, Mr. Foote said to the boy: "It's not sundown yet, son. You'll have to go back to the plow."

Gritting his teeth, young Gaston stayed with it until almost sundown. He said it was the hardest week's work he ever did in one day.

Often through the years, he later related, when things were hard and he was tempted to give up, he said he seemed to feel his dad's hand on his shoulder and his gentle voice saying, "Go back to the plow, son—it isn't sundown yet."

The temptation to quit is one of the severest temptations any Christian ever faces. The cost of the Christian life seems too great for us to pay, and, poor weaklings that we are, we are sorely tempted to give it all up and quit.

Some of the Jewish believers to whom this letter was addressed were facing that very temptation. They had professed faith in Jesus as the Messiah. They had abandoned the faith of their fathers and the Temple sacrifices in which they had been reared. Because of this, some of their own people were making it hard for them to remain faithful to Jesus.

"Is it worth it?" they were asking. "Have we only been carried away by our enthusiasm to an empty and vain hope in this Jesus? Is He really the Messiah?"

The Holy Spirit knew their hearts. He knew their fears and how greatly they were tempted to quit, so He caused this epistle to be written to encourage them not to abandon their faith in Christ.

The Holy Spirit tells us in this great passage that when we are tempted to quit to remember some things, and we will discover a new strength that will enable us to hold on and not quit Jesus.

    I. Remember the joy of your conversion (v. 32).
      1. Remember the gracious Friend you met.
      2. Remember the great change He brought.
    II. Remember the promise of heaven (vv. 34-36).
      1. Remember that better days are coming (v. 34).
      2. Remember the reward that lies ahead (v. 35).
      3. Remember the promise Jesus has made (v. 36).
   III. Remember the promise of Christ's coming (v. 37).
      1. It won't be long.
      2. It is certain.

IV. Remember the disappointment we would be if we turned away from Jesus (vv. 38-39).
   1. A great disappointment to our Lord (v. 38).
   2. A great disappointment to ourselves (v. 39).

Conclusion:

In a sermon titled "The Door to Heaven," Dr. George W. Truett, for forty-seven years pastor of First Baptist Church, Dallas, Texas, told about an army surgeon who came upon a wounded soldier at Gettysburg.

Seeing a man down in a trench, the doctor looked at him from horseback and decided that he was already dead. But as he looked more closely, a faint smile came on the dying soldier's face.

Dismounting and kneeling by the side of the wounded soldier, the doctor faintly heard the boy whisper, "Here!" "Here!"

Shaking the boy so as to arouse him, the doctor asked the wounded soldier why he was answering "here"? And the boy faintly replied, "They were calling the roll in heaven, and I was answering to my name."[1]

It has never been easy to be a Christian. And most believers would confess that at one time or another they have been tempted to quit. But it will be worth it all when we see Jesus.

---

1. From *20 Centuries of Great Preaching* by Clyde Fant and Bill Pinson, vol. VIII, pp. 158-159, copyright © 1971; used by permission of Word Books, Publisher, Waco, Texas 76796.

41
The Book that Is Different

Scripture: *2 Timothy 3:14-17*

Introduction:

A young Christian sailor who was stationed in New Orleans during World War II had the good habit of closing each day with Scripture reading and prayer.

Early one morning after he had spent the night on duty, he picked up his Bible and began to read the twenty-third Psalm. The thought occurred to him, as he was reading, to tap out the passage in code to see how many ships at sea would pick up the signal.

Carefully he tapped out the psalm: "Surely goodness and mercy shall follow me all the days of my life: and I will dwell in the house of the Lord for ever."

When he had finished, he was amazed as he heard sixteen ships at sea send back an "Amen" to the psalm.

What is this Book that has stimulated so much interest for so many years—that has been a best-seller for decades? What is this Book that has been loved devotedly and clung to tenaciously by millions of believers for centuries?

It is the Bible. It is the Book that is different.

> Century follows century—There it stands.
> Empires rise and fall and are forgotten—There it stands.
> Dynasty succeeds dynasty—There it stands.
> Kings are crowned and uncrowned—There it stands.
> Emperors decree its extermination—There it stands.
> Atheists rail against it—There it stands.
> Agnostics smile cynically—There it stands.

Profane prayerless punsters caricature it—There it stands.

Unbelief abandons it—There it stands.

Higher critics deny its claim to inspiration—There it stands.

The flames are kindled about it—There it stands.

The tooth of time gnaws but makes no dent in it—There it stands.

Infidels predict its abandonment—There it stands.

Modernism tries to explain it away—There it stands.[1]

I. It is an ancient Book.

Perhaps as many as fifty authors worked over a period of 1,500 years in writing it. But its Author is the Holy Spirit.

1. This ancient Book has been loved for centuries (v. 15).

"Holy Scriptures" refers to the Old Testament because that was all the Scriptures Timothy had. But the New Testament is now a part of holy Scripture for Christians (Heb. 1:1).

2. This ancient Book is a revelation of God (Heb. 1:1-2). "God . . . spake in times past unto the fathers, . . . Hath in these last days spoken unto us by his Son."

II. It is a holy Book.

The Bible is not such a Book as man would have written if he could, or could have written if he would.

1. It is sacred (v. 15).

"The holy scriptures." The Greek words mean "hallowed, holy, divine writings."

2. It is inspired (v. 16).

"All scripture is given by inspiration of God." *Inspiration* is a combination of two words which mean: "God breathed." Every particle of Scripture is "breathed upon" by almighty God (see 2 Pet. 1:20-21).

III. It is a precious Book.

"And the word of the Lord was precious in those days" (1 Sam. 3:1).

1. It is precious because of the Person it reveals (v. 15).

2. It is precious because of the promise it gives (v. 15).
3. It is precious because of the profit it produces (v. 16).

Conclusion:

The greatest violin maker of history was Antonio Stradivari. When Stradivari died at ninety-four, family and friends looked through the papers in his workshop to see if they could find the secret to the unique instruments Stradivari made. But all was in vain.

Many years after his death, Stradivari's great-grandson found some of the old master's papers in an old Bible. The papers were written in Stradivari's own handwriting and were dated 1704. In those papers the formula for the varnish Stradivari used was discovered, along with other secrets about the glue, wood, and other materials used by the master.

But the great-grandson told no one what he had found. And he carried Stradivari's secret with him to the grave.

But more than Stradivari's secret formulas for making violins can be found in the Bible. In it are the secrets of life, death, and eternity. And the one who reads this sacred Book and discovers these precious secrets cannot keep them to oneself.

---

1. Walter B. Knight, *Knight's Book of New Illustrations* Wm. B. Eerdmans Publishing Company, 1956), p. 26. Used by permission. By Rev. A. Z. Conrad, Park Street Church, Boston.

42
The Choice that Counts

Scripture: Joshua 24:14-16

Introduction:

There are a great many things in life we do not understand. Some are important, and some are not so important. This is one of those interesting but not so important things.

It is easy to understand why silver dollars migrate to Las

Vegas, Nevada, the gambling capital of the world. But why are there more half-dollars in New York City than any other place? And why do more pennies wind up in Pittsburgh and Dallas than in any other cities in the United States? And why do Louisville, Nashville, and Baltimore have a larger supply of dimes and nickels than other cities?

There is no need to write the Treasury Department and ask them why. They are stumped, too.

There are a great many things in life we do not understand, but we perfectly understand the words of Joshua, "Choose you this day whom ye will serve" (v. 15).

His words are clear, sharp, and easily understood. Joshua was talking about the choice that counts.

This matter of forsaking evil and choosing to serve the Lord is the most important choice a person will ever face.

   I. It is a positive choice.
      1. To do what is right (v. 14).
         "Now therefore fear the Lord, and serve him in sincerity and truth." (v. 14).
      2. To forsake what is wrong.
         "Put away the gods which your father served on the other side of the flood, and in Egypt" (v. 14).
  II. It is a personal choice.
      1. You must make it.
         "And if it seem evil unto *you* . . . choose *you* . . . as for *me* and *my* house, *we* will serve the Lord" (v. 15).
      2. Your interests are at stake (v. 15).
         Your choice will determine whom you will serve, the quality of life you will live, and where you will spend eternity.
 III. It is a pressing choice.
      1. It demands immediate attention (v. 15).
         "Choose you *this day* whom ye will serve" (v. 15).
      2. It demands immediate action (v. 15).
         "*Choose* . . . we will serve the Lord" (v. 15).

Conclusion:

Abraham Lincoln was one of my heroes. He was shot by John Wilkes Booth on April 14, 1865, in Ford's Theater in Washington, DC. He died the following morning at 7:22 AM.

According to a report that was released several years ago, Abraham Lincoln intended to join the New York Avenue Presbyterian Church in Washington on April 18, 1865. The stated clerk of the Washington church, Frank S. Edington, wrote a book on Lincoln that declared Lincoln was to be admitted to church membership upon the confession of his faith.

Before Lincoln moved to Washington, he attended the First Presbyterian Church of Springfield, Illinois. But Lincoln was never a member of that church or any other church. Although he had been assigned a pew in the Washington church, attended services regularly, and contributed to the church, Lincoln was never a member. But he was, no doubt, a believer.

Whether it can be believed is debatable, but according to Edington, Lincoln would have joined the church if he had lived only four more days.

The choice that counts—accepting Jesus as one's Savior and making an open confession of that faith—is a decision that cannot be delayed.

43
The Courage of Great Convictions

Scripture: 1 Kings 18:36-40

Introduction:

William Booth was a Methodist minister who had strange ideas about the Lord's work. Taking the gospel to London's down-and-outs in the red-light districts, Booth fell under the criticism of his fellow ministers and was called on the carpet at the church's annual conference in Liverpool.

He asked to be set free from his pastoral responsibilities so he could pursue his innovative work full-time, but his church superiors wouldn't go along with him.

Booth was instructed in the Liverpool conference to confine

his ministry to the small church to which he had been assigned. But Catherine, his wife, stood in the gallery and boldly called out: "Never!"

On the floor below, Booth jumped to his feet, waved his hat in the air, and met Catherine at the foot of the stairs. Leaving the conference that had tried to confine the gospel to the respectable areas of London, the two of them walked out into Liverpool's damp air to found the Salvation Army which ministers to derelicts and ne'er-do-wells around the world.

When Booth was later asked where he was going to get ministers for his Salvation Army, he replied: "Out of the saloons."

Wealth, personality, ability, and determination are important. But they are not the things that necessarily make one great. It is what we believe that makes us great. Men and women driven by great convictions are the people who live nobly and courageously.

Elijah was such a person. A prophet of God who lived nine centuries before Jesus, Elijah's mountainlike life magnificently testifies to the courage of great convictions.

What convictions are these that equip one to live nobly and worthily? Though, no doubt, they are numerous, I will mention only three.

I. We must believe in God.
    1.   That He is with us in our endeavors.
        "Lord God of Abraham, Isaac, and of Israel" (v. 36).
        As God was with the patriarchs, so He is with us.
    2.   That He is dependable.
        "Let it be known this day that thou art God in Israel" (v. 36). Challenged by Baal's prophets, Elijah called on Israel's God and trusted in the divine dependability.
    3.   That He will hear our prayers.
        "Hear me, O Lord, hear me, that this people may know that thou art the Lord God" (v. 37).
    4.   That He is able.
        "Then the fire of the Lord fell" (v. 38).
II. We must believe in ourselves.
        This was Elijah's finest hour. His self-confidence was obvious. Ralph Waldo Emerson once said, "They can conquer who believe they can."
    1.   We must believe God has chosen us for our task.

"Let it be known . . . I am thy servant" (v. 36).
2. We must believe we are acting obediently.
"I have done all these things at thy word" (v. 36).
3. We must then act courageously.
"Elijah came unto all the people, and said, How long halt ye between two opinions? If the Lord be God, follow him" (v. 21).
III. We must believe in our cause.
1. That it is a right cause.
"Let it be known this day that thou art God in Israel" (v. 36).
2. That it is a worthy cause.
"And he repaired the altar of the Lord that was broken down" (v. 30).
"And with the stones he made an altar in the name of the Lord" (v. 32).
3. That it is a lasting cause.
When Elijah turned the people back to God, the cause to which the prophet had given himself was a cause that would never die: "The Lord, he is the God; the Lord, he is the God" (v. 39).

Conclusion:

Davy Crockett, the Tennessee frontiersman who became a legend at the Alamo, was fond of saying, "Be sure you're right, then go ahead!"

What one believes determines what one does. Being right in our convictions about God, ourselves, and our cause puts us on the road to successful living.

44
The Cupboard That's
Never Bare

Scripture: 1 Kings 17:8-24

Introduction:

Among the nursery rhymes that many of us learned at our mother's knees is this favorite:

> Old mother Hubbard Went to the cupboard
>   To fetch her poor dog a bone,
> But when she came there,
>   The cupboard was bare
> And so the poor dog had none.

Poor Old Mother Hubbard's cupboard was bare. But there is a cupboard that's never bare.

Elijah the prophet had warned wicked King Ahab that God's judgment was about to fall on Israel. Ahab had led the nation into idolatry, and God had had enough. Having delivered his message, Elijah was told by the Lord to go out to the brook Cherith and stay there. Water from the brook would quench the prophet's thirst, and the ravens would feed him, God promised.

But the drought prophesied by Elijah dried up the brook, and the Lord told Elijah to go to Zarephath where a "widow woman" would take care of him.

Elijah did as God commanded, but when he got to Zarephath, he found the poor widow in worse shape than he was. But even in that trying situation, God proved His faithfulness. Consider the following in this passage.

    I. The timing of God (v. 8).

        1. God doesn't get in a hurry.

        2. God's time may not be our time.

3. God's time is best.
II. The means of God (v. 9).
1. He can use common things.
2. He can use common people.
III. The priority of God (vv. 10-11).
1. God must come before self.
2. God must come before family.
IV. The promise of God (vv. 13-15).
1. We may not understand it (v. 13).
2. We must act on it (vv. 14-15).
V. The provision of God (v. 16).
1. His provision is dependable.
2. His provision is sufficient.
VI. The grace of God (vv. 17-24).
1. Even as we serve Him, trials may come (v. 17).
2. But as we serve Him, His grace is sufficient (vv. 19-24).

Conclusion:

Christopher Columbus was discouraged and all but defeated. Although he had tried hard, he hadn't been able to find a sponsor for his trip to the new world.

Stopping one day at Granada to get a drink of water, Columbus met a monk from a nearby convent who gave Columbus a drink and listened to his tale of discouragement. As a result of their providential encounter, the monk spoke to Queen Isabella, and she provided the funds Columbus needed.

As God used a chance meeting with a monk and a request for a glass of water to open a new world to Europe, so God used a widow and a loaf of bread to care for His prophet.

Though our resources may be exhausted by life's demands, we serve One whose strength is never exhausted and whose cupboard is never bare.

45
The Divine Dreamer

Scripture: Jeremiah 18:1-4

Introduction:

American poet Edwin Markham once said that all that we glory in was once a dream.

By that he meant that before anything becomes a reality, it is first a thought, a desire, an ambition.

Without glorious dreams, there are no glorious deeds.

A young, redheaded man sat down and began to write. He was not yet old enough to serve as president of the United States, but for some time he had been dreaming about freedom. The result of Thomas Jefferson's dream was the Declaration of Independence, one of the noblest documents ever penned.

Another young man walked in the woods of his native Germany. There, in the wide-open spaces, he heard symphonies of music rustling among the leaves. Even when he lost his hearing at forty-two, his ambition to write deathless music wouldn't die. His name was Ludwig van Beethoven, and he was a great dreamer.

Another young man labored over an odd piece of machinery. When his steam engine finally coughed into life, he told his friends that what they saw with their physical eyes he had long ago seen with his mind's eye. His name was James Watts, and his steam engine revolutionized industry. He was a great dreamer.

But Almighty God, too, is a great dreamer. Long before He created man and the world and everything in it, the thought and desire were in the heart of the eternal God. And in Eden the divine dream became a living reality.

Long ago, Jeremiah the prophet was exposed to the dream of

the divine dreamer. He met Him in a strange place, down at the lowly potter's house. But there Jeremiah learned a profound and unforgettable lesson. As he watched the potter at work at his wheel, he felt the heartbeat of the divine dreamer as that dream became a reality.

But as the prophet watched, the dream of the creator was marred, and re-creation had to take place.

There are three stages in this drama that shows the divine dreamer at work.

I. God created us (vv. 1-3).

The potter is God. The vessel being created represented Israel and, today, all humanity. It is a quaint picture that taught Jeremiah a profound lesson about God's creative power. It is the divine explanation for life (Gen. 2:7).

II. Sin desecrated us (v. 4).

"And the vessel that he made of clay was marred in the hand of the potter" (v. 4).

God's magnificient dream was marred. As the potter worked on the soft clay, the vessel he was making was ruined. It is a picture of sin entering into the human heart, desecrating the divine creation (Gen. 3).

III. Christ recreated us (v. 4b).

"So he made it again another vessel, as seemed good to the potter to make it" (v. 4). It is a picture of God's love for sinful mankind and His refusal to give up on them. When God's original dream failed because of human sin, God sent Christ who through His death, burial, and resurrection, coupled with our faith, recreates us in His own image.

Conclusion:

Anatole France, in his novel *The Procurator of Judea*, pictured Pilate meeting Lamia on the Bay of Naples. The two old friends talked about things they experienced many years earlier.

Lamia asked Pilate if he ever heard the name of Jesus while he was in Israel. Lamia told Pilate that Jesus had been crucified for some kind of crime.

Scratching his forehead, Pilate responded, "Jesus of Nazareth? I cannot call Him to mind."

Ask anyone in the first century, in the Middle Ages, or in the present century, who has ever met Jesus Christ if he remembers Him, and the inevitable answer will be: "Jesus? Yes, indeed, I know Him very well. He is the One who gave me a second chance."

"The vessel he made of clay was marred in the hands of the potter: so he made it again another vessel, as seemed good to the potter to make it" (v. 4).

46
The Glory of a Great Faith

Scripture: 1 Samuel 17:44-51

Introduction:

As every student of church history knows, Martin Luther was not always right. His attitude toward other believers was sometimes much less than what it should have been. But for all of his contradictions, Martin Luther was a great Christian.

Look at him as he stood in the presence of Emperor Charles. Luther knew full well that he was bringing down the wrath of both the state and church against himself, but he could not deny his convictions. "Here I stand," he said. "God help me. I cannot do otherwise."

As Luther journeyed out of his own spiritual darkness into the light, he was moved by the glory of a great faith. The Bible had come alive for Luther. Justification by grace through faith was a discovery that changed the course of his life and the direction of history as well. A great man whose life was often contradictory, Luther still possessed an undying faith in Jesus Christ.

This was the same kind of faith David possessed as he stood before Goliath, the Philistine giant. The boasting of Goliath had stopped Israel's army. Saul and his men were cowering in fear and defeat. But in Israel's moment of greatest need, God raised up a shepherd boy who possessed a faith sufficient for the crisis.

As we think about the glory of a great faith, look at these three thoughts.

    I. An impossible situation (vv. 8-11).
        1. They try us (v. 10).
        2. They trouble us (v. 11, "dismayed").
        3. They frighten us (v. 11).
   II. A courageous faith (vv. 32-37).
        1. God will use it (v. 32).
        2. God will bless it (vv. 33-37).
  III. A great victory (vv. 40-50).
        1. God often uses common means to give victory (vv. 40-50).
        2. God blesses faith in giving victory (vv. 32,37,49).
        3. God gets glory in giving victory (v. 46).

Conclusion:

Truly great men and women of history have not been defeated by difficulties. Alexander the Great heard of India's wealth. Rivers, mountains, and strong nations held no terror for him. Even the feared Kyber Pass would not stop Alexander.

Caesar determined to conquer Britain. A grueling march would not stop Caesar.

Napoleon saw Italy but not the Alps. Washington saw the Hessians but not the frozen Delaware. Lincoln saw a nation divided, but the greatness of his cause nerved his arm.

And David saw Israel paralyzed by a boastful giant. But when David exercised his faith and put himself at God's disposal, God honored his faith.

William H. Bathurst summed up the glory of a great faith in these four lines:

        O, for a faith that will not shrink,
          Tho' pressed by ev'ry foe,
      That will not tremble on the brink
          Of any earthly woe.

47
The Great Commission

Scripture: *Matthew 28:18-20*

Introduction:

The text upon which this message is based is commonly called the Great Commission. Very few passages in the New Testament are as well known. Every Sunday School pupil is exposed to it before he or she has progressed very far. Every child and young person who has ever been a member of one of the church's missionary groups is compelled to learn it. It is, indeed, one of the most-quoted passages in the Word of God.

It was the Great Commission, given by the risen Lord, that caused the ancient church to break out of its channels and flood the world with its message of hope. It was the Great Commission burning in the hearts of missionaries Adoniram Judson, Luther Rice, and William Carey that gave rise to the modern mission movement.

This may be Christ's last-spoken word to the church. He is the Holy Victor. Having died for the sins of the world, He has been raised from the dead by the power of God. Having conquered death, man's last enemy and greatest fear, Jesus now tells His disciples to take the good news to all the nations. It is an imperative command that the church cannot neglect.

As we look at these three verses, let us note:

I. The authority Jesus possesses (v. 18).
    1. Personal authority (v. 18).
    2. Pervasive authority (v. 18).

II. The work Jesus gives (v. 19-20).
    1. Is to disciple (v. 19).
    2. Is to baptize (v. 19).
    3. Is to teach (v. 20).

III. The companionship Jesus promises (v. 20).
   1. Personal companionship (v. 20).
   2. Permanent companionship (v. 20).

Conclusion:

In carrying out his Lord's Great Commission, William Carey gave rise to the modern mission movement. The first of the great modern missionaries, Carey set sail from his native England in June 1793. Five months later he landed at Calcutta. As Carey left England and his friends and loved ones, his last words to them were: "Yonder in India is a gold mine. I will descend and dig, but you at home must hold the ropes."

And since Carey landed in Calcutta in 1793, untold thousands of missionaries have followed in his wake in obedience to the Great Commission of the Savior.

48
The Highway to Happiness

Scripture: Matthew 5:1-12

Introduction:

The Sermon on the Mount is one of the greatest pieces of literature known to mankind. It has been called the Magna Charta of the kingdom and the manifesto of the King. In the Sermon on the Mount, we have the essence, the core, of Christ's teachings.

In this marvelous message, Christ shows His disciples the highway to happiness. And He promises that all who faithfully walk this highway will possess a happiness the world cannot take away.

Because of the length of the Sermon on the Mount, this outline is confined to the first twelve verses, which are commonly known as the Beatitudes. In them, Jesus shows us some of the blessings that will be ours as we walk the highway to happiness.

I. This highway is open to all.
1. The poor can travel it (v. 3).
2. The sad can travel it (v. 4).
3. The humble can travel it (v. 5).
4. The needy can travel it (v. 5).
5. Etc., etc. (vv. 6-11).
II. This highway is well marked.
To walk this highway one must:
1. Shun pride (vv. 3-5).
2. Want to walk it (v. 6).
3. Practice mercy (v. 7).
4. Live purely (v. 8).
5. Etc., etc. (vv. 9-12).
III. This highway leads to pleasant places.
1. Personal peace (v. 4).
2. Personal victory (v. 5).
3. Personal fulfillment (v. 6).
4. Personal satisfaction (v. 7-12).

Conclusion:

John A. Redhead in his book *Living All Your Life* said that there are three kinds of happiness: pleasure, joy, and blessings.

Pleasure comes from satisfying our physical senses. Joy comes from our association with others. But happiness results from a right relationship with God.

Quoting H. H. Farmer, who was a professor at Cambridge University, Redhead concluded: "The true blessedness of life is in doing God's will and in the fellowship with Him that such brings."

In His Sermon on the Mount, Jesus said the same thing. In simple steps that any believer can follow, Jesus showed us how to walk the highway to happiness.

49
The Love of God

Scripture: John 3:16

Introduction:

How many times have you heard the expression, "Thanks a million"? We use it often to express deep gratitude to someone who has done something nice for us.

When I was pastor in Lubbock, Texas, I took one of our sons into the orthodontist's office, and seeing a book there with a rather unusual title, I picked it up to examine it more closely. On examination, I found that the book contained 1,323 pages, and on each page the word *thanks* occurred 756 times!

That's all there was to the book. The word *thanks* was written one million times! And, appropriately, the title of the book was *Thanks a Million!*

The book had been given to the doctor by Dub Rogers, the mayor of Lubbock. The doctor, in some thoughtful way, had so befriended the mayor that in a very unique way the mayor said to him, "Thanks a million!"

If it were possible for us to thank Jesus a million times for what He has done for us, it would still not be enough. But that's what John 3:16 says.

Look at this simple "Thanks-a-million" outline on the love of God.

   I. The excellence of that love.
      "God so loved."
  II. The expanse of that love.
      "The world."
 III. The expense of that love.
      "That he gave his only begotten Son."
  IV. The extravagance of that love.
         "Should not perish, but have everlasting life."

Conclusion:
Conclusion:

When Felix Mendelssohn, the great composer, fell gloriously in love with the girl who later became his wife, he wrote to his sister Rebecca: "I am more desperately in love than I ever was in my life before, and I do not know what to do. . . . I have not an idea whether she likes me or not, and I do not know what to do to make her like me. . . . When away from her . . . I am always sad . . . O, Rebecca! What shall I do?"

What shall we do in response to love so great?

50
The Love of God

Scripture: Jeremiah 31:3

Introduction:

An American tourist who was visiting Seville, Spain, became lost in the city and couldn't find the way back to his hotel. Stopping a woman on the street, he asked her the way to the hotel, and she replied: "Find the Calle Amor de Dios (Street of the Love of God) and follow it. It will take you straight to your hotel."

There's a lesson for us in this simple illustration. The thing that men and women need to discover more than anything else is that God loves them. When they discover they are loved by God, it will make a difference in their lives. Experiencing the love of God is the road that leads to happiness, peace, freedom from guilt, and joyous living.

This passage of Scripture says a great deal about the love of God. Let us take a careful look at Jeremiah's verse and see what he says about this marvelous subject.

    I. God's love is personal.

        "*I* have loved thee."

    II. God's love is certain.

        "I *have* loved thee."

    III. God's love is directed.

"I have loved *thee*."

IV. God's love is eternal.

"I have loved thee with an *everlasting* love."

V. God's love is far-reaching.

"The Lord hath appeared *of old* unto me."

"The Lord appeared to him *from afar*" (RSV).

VI. God's love is powerful.

"Therefore with lovingkindness *have I drawn thee*."

Conclusion:

Roy Angell in his book *Baskets of Silver* told about an experiment carried out at the Kellogg Sanitarium in Battle Creek, Michigan.

A puppy was found hanging around the buildings at the sanitarium and was brought inside. Everybody in the sanitarium fell in love with the little dog. He was so full of affection that he nearly wagged his tail off every time somebody spoke to him.

Dr. Caroline Geisel decided to experiment on the little dog. Taking him into the operating room, Dr. Geisel made an incision in one of his hind legs. The tissue was red and healthy looking.

Binding up the incision, she passed the word around the sanitarium that no one was to pay any attention to the puppy or to speak kindly to him for six weeks. They fed the little dog, but nobody petted him or showed any affection for him.

In a few days, he had become the most forlorn, pitiful little dog imaginable. His little tail dragged the ground, and he stayed to himself as though he were afraid to come out among his friends.

When they took the puppy back into the operating room at the end of six weeks and made a small incision in one of his legs, they found that the once-healthy-looking muscle and tissue was now brown in color. And the wound took a long time to heal.

They then gave the puppy the first-class treatment. Everybody spoke to him and petted him when they met him. Soon his ears perked up and his tail began to wag and the brightness came back to his eyes. And when they took him to the operating room the next time, the muscle and tissues were pink and healthy looking again.

Dr. Geisel concluded from her experiments that love is essential for happiness and good health. Without love, life loses its vitality and beauty.

If the love of a sanitarium staff would do that for a forlorn little puppy, imagine what the love of God will do for a person when that person's life is opened up to Jesus Christ.

51
The Man Who Made the Wrong Choice

Scripture: Mark 10:17-22

Introduction:

The year I was graduated from the seminary, I was pastor of a church in the oil fields of east Texas.

One morning when I went to the post office, I looked off in the distance and saw a huge, billowing, cloud of black smoke. When an ambulance and a fire truck rushed by the post office with sirens blaring, I knew there had been an accident. Thinking that some of the men in our church might have been involved in the accident, I quickly drove out to the edge of town where an oil rig was on fire.

A crew had been working on an old well when they hit a gas pocket, and a spark ignited a fire. And Cozelle White was high above the floor of the rig, working in the crow's nest.

When a spark ignited the gas, White started down, urging the men on the floor to keep the fire extinguishers on the flame. But as he got within about fifteen feet of the floor of the rig, the flames and heat were so intense that he started back up. The flames overcame him, and he fell to his death on the rig floor.

White was within fifteen feet of safety, but he made the wrong choice.

In this text of Scripture from Mark's Gospel, Jesus talks about another man who made the wrong choice. His name is not known to us.

I. He came to the right person (Acts 4:12; John 8:24; 14:6; Luke 19:10; Acts 16:31).
II. He came at the right time.
He came when the Holy Spirit was drawing him (John 6:44; 12:32; Rev. 3:20; 2 Cor. 6:2).
III. He asked the right question.
He asked, "Good Master, what shall I do that I may inherit eternal life?" (v. 17).
The words *eternal life* appear about thirty times in the New Testament. Our question concerning eternal life is the most important question we will ever ask.
IV. He got the right answer (Mark 10:18-22; John 3:16; Rom. 10:9-10; and John 5:24).
V. But he made the wrong choice (Mark 10:22; John 3:18).

Conclusion:

The city of Johnstown, Pennsylvania, was settled in 1793. A dam was built in 1889, twelve miles east of the city, to control flood waters. But on May 31, 1889 the reservoir burst and the waters rushed down the valley killing more than two thousand people. Property worth more than ten million dollars was also lost.

Civil engineers had examined the dam and had warned the people of Johnstown that the dam was unsafe. But the people failed to heed the warning of the engineers.

Not more than fifteen days after engineers had warned the citizens, a boy galloped into town on his horse, shouting, "Run for your lives! The dam has broken!"

But, again, the people didn't believe the warning and thirty minutes later the town and more than two thousand people were destroyed.

Delay is always dangerous. But to delay in making the right choice about Jesus Christ and life eternal can be the most expensive wrong choice a person will ever make.

52
The Man Who Sold Out

Scripture: Matthew 26:14-16

Introduction:

Who do you suppose is the most despised man in American history?

How about Benedict Arnold?

When the colonies rebelled against English tyranny, Benedict Arnold was a successful and prosperous businessman in New Haven, Connecticut. Shortly after the beginning of hostilities, Arnold raised a body of volunteers and received a colonel's commission in the fledgling army.

Because Arnold distinguished himself as a soldier, he had the complete confidence of General George Washington. As a reward for his meritorious service for the cause of freedom, Arnold was made the head of the government in Philadelphia. But because of his imprudence in the administration of his duties, Arnold was court-martialed and severely reprimanded.

The reprimand deeply humiliated the proud Arnold, and he determined to get even. Opening communications with Sir Henry Clinton, the British commander, Arnold made a pact to surrender West Point to the enemy. The attempt was discovered and thwarted, and Arnold fled to the English side where he was appointed a brigadier general in His Majesty's service.

History remembers Benedict Arnold as the man who sold out. But in this text of Scripture, I wish to direct your attention to another man who sold out to the enemy. It is the sad biography of Judas Iscariot, a disciple of Jesus.

    I. He sold out his best friend (vv. 14-16).

                Judas sold Jesus for thirty pieces of silver, about eighteen dollars in our money.

II. He sold out his most-glorious opportunity.

Judas was one of the twelve disciples and was so trusted that he was chosen treasurer of the apostolic band (John 12:6).

Concerning opportunity, the eloquent Greek Demosthenes said, "Small opportunities are often the beginning of great enterprises."

Concerning opportunity, Abraham Lincoln said, "I happen, temporarily, to occupy this White House. I'm a living witness that any one of your children may look to come here as my father's child has."

But the opportunity that Jesus gave to Judas was the greatest opportunity of all. It was the opportunity to follow Jesus on earth and live with Jesus eternally.

III. He sold out his good name.

Judas means "praised." One wonders what high expectations his parents had of him when he was born and as they praised God for their blessing. But his name has become a byword and an expression for all that is contemptible.

IV. He sold out a blessed fellowship.

Judas gave up the fellowship of Jesus, Peter, James, John, Matthew, and others, for the fellowship of the betrayers and slayers of our Lord.

V. He sold out a heavenly home.

Did Judas go to heaven? The answer is given by our Lord in John 17:12. Read how Judas died in Acts 1:16-20.

Conclusion:

Judas is a strong warning to each of us. He lived, slept, and walked with Jesus for three years. He heard the Master's matchless messages firsthand. But impentitent Judas never received Jesus as his personal Savior.

It is possible for one to know *about* Jesus and not know Him as Savior and Lord.

53
The Most-Frequently Asked Question

Scripture: Job 14:1-15

Introduction:

According to Ian Macpherson in his book *The Burden of the Lord,* the visitor to the Egyptological section of the British Museum in London can see a strange sight. There is a stone coffin, Macpherson said, containing the body of an Egyptian who died 3,000 years ago. Crudely embalmed but marvelously preserved in the dry sand in which it is interred, the body is still clearly visible after thirty centuries. Buried in a crouching position, resembling a huge question mark, the body seems to be asking the centuries-old question of Job, "If a man die, shall he live again?"

This is the most frequently asked question of all history. It has been asked more than any other question formed by the lips of mankind. It was first asked by Adam and Eve when Cain slew Abel. It has been asked by every generation of people since that time. And when the last human being comes to die, as he or she breathes out the last breath, the question of Job shall still be upon those dying lips: "If a man die, shall he live again?"

As we consider the most frequently asked question, consider:
- I. A statement about life (vv. 1-2).
  - 1. Life is filled with trouble (v. 1).
  - 2. Life is as fragile as a flower (v. 2).
  - 3. Life fades as a shadow (v. 2).
- II. A lamentation about death (vv. 5-12).
  - 1. Death is certain (v. 5).
  - 2. Life has set boundaries (v. 5).
  - 3. Death's finality is disturbing (vv. 7-12).

III. A question about resurrection (vv. 13-15).
   1. Will God remember us after we die? (v. 13).
   2. Will God change us after we die? (v. 14).

Conclusion:

William Sydney Porter was an American writer who used the pen name O. Henry. Born in 1862, O. Henry died in 1910. During his lifetime, he wrote nearly 250 works of fiction.

It is reported that when O. Henry was on his deathbed he exclaimed to his nurse, "Nurse, light me a candle; I am afraid to go home in the dark."

We have more knowledge of life, death, and eternity than Job had. Because of the death, burial, and resurrection of Jesus Christ, we know now that there is life beyond the grave and a resurrection that awaits us all.

If Christ is our Savior, we do not go home in the dark. We walk life's last journey with Him who is the Light of the world and who turns all of our questions about eternity into periods.

54
The Sunshine and the Shadows

Scripture: Genesis 39

Introduction:

William Barclay, the late Anglican minister and theologian, told in his autobiography about the tragic death of his young daughter.

Some time after the tragedy, the British Broadcasting Company asked Barclay to speak to the nation on the miracles of Jesus and how those miracles apply to modern life.

Barclay said he was glad to do it because he always felt that we ought to regard Jesus not so much as a person who did things long ago but as One who is active with His people today.

In the last radio broadcast, Barclay was interviewed by the

announcer who asked how he had come to the conclusion that the miracles of Jesus are so applicable to modern life.

In answering the announcer's question, Barclay related the tragic drowning of his daughter some years earlier. She was only twenty-one, and on the day she was to have been married both she and her fiance were drowned in a boating accident.

God did not stop the drowning, but He did still the storm in Barclay's own heart. And because of Christ's presence with them to give them peace, he and Mrs. Barclay were able to survive the severest ordeal of their lives.

One of the most unique people I ever met was Norman Vincent Peale. My wife and I heard him one Sunday when he was pastor of New York City's Marble Collegiate Church. We had an appointment with him after the service, and he shared with us some of the optimism and faith that permeates all the books he wrote.

Peale says in one of his books that he learned a thing from his friend Jim Johnson, a hotel operator in Harrisburg, Pennsylvania, which he never forgot. "I never knew a storm that didn't blow itself out," Johnson told Peale.

And that's true. Life is a mixture of sunshine and shadows. If the sun shines today, the shadows will come tomorrow. If the shadows darken our pathway today, the sun will shine tomorrow. Life is a combination of sunshine and shadows.

Young Joseph learned this the hard way. When he was only seventeen, he went out to check on his half brothers who were tending sheep on the plains of Dothan. Jealous of Joseph, the brothers sold Joseph into slavery for twenty pieces of silver.

But God was in it. God didn't initiate Joseph's kidnapping and slavery, but He used them for His own glory, for Joseph's good, and to save Israel from starvation.

Joseph's life is a marvelous commentary on the New Testament statement of Paul: "And we know that all things work together for good to them that love God, to them who are the called according to his purpose" (Rom. 8:28).

As we face life with its sunshine and shadows, let us keep these truths in mind:

    I. The Lord is with us.
        1. He is with us in our dark days (v. 1).
        2. He is with us to bless us (vv. 2-6).
        3. He is with us to use us (vv. 3-4).

II. Our faith will be tested.
1. Temptation will come (v. 7).
2. God will strengthen us in it (v. 8).
3. We can use it as a testimony (v. 9).
4. It can ruin us (vv. 16-20).
5. It can make us (vv. 21-23).
III. We can be overcomers.
1. Faith is required (vv. 2,9).
2. Convictions are required (v. 9).
3. Courage is required (v. 10).
4. Action is required (v. 12).

Conclusion:

The late Martin Niemöller was a Jewish Christian who survived the horrors of Dachau Prison during World War II. In those prison camps set up by Hitler, more than six million Jews were slain.

Before Pastor Niemöller was arrested, he had stood courageously against the German dictator. Because of this, he was thrown into the prison and, for months on end, he was kept in solitary confinement. The sight of men and women walking to their death and the stench of burning flesh, tormented him every day.

But God spared Niemöller, and after the war he came to America. On one occasion, when he was being interviewed by a Chicago radio station, the announcer asked Niemöller how he kept his sanity. Pastor Niemöller replied that one doesn't know how much one can stand until one has been put to the test. "You can stand far more than you think," he said. "You are much stronger than you think you are if God is dwelling in your life."

It is true! Joseph's experience and our experience confirm it.

55
The Wonder of It All

Scripture: *Ephesians 1:3-14*

Introduction:
"Longfellow could take a worthless sheet of paper, write a poem on it, and make it worth $6,000—that's genius.

"Rockefeller could sign his name to a piece of paper and make it worth a million dollars—*that's capital.*

"Uncle Sam can take gold, stamp an eagle on it, and make it worth $20.00—*that's money.*

"A mechanic can take material that is worth only $5.00 and make it worth $50.00—*that's skill.*

"An artist can take a fifty-cent piece of canvas, paint a picture on it, and make it worth $1,000—*that's art.*

"God can take a worthless, sinful life, wash it in the blood of Christ, put His Spirit in it, and make it a blessing to humanity —*that's salvation.*"[1]

As Paul wrote the Ephesian believers, he was marveling at the wonder of God's grace that had brought Paul and his readers out of their sins, into the light of God's love.

As Paul mused on the wonder of it all, he shared with us some unforgettable truths about the grace of God.

I. We were divinely chosen by grace.
    1. We were chosen in Christ.
        "He hath chosen us in him" (v. 4).
    2. We were chosen from eternity.
        "chosen . . . before the foundation of the world" (v. 4).
    3. We were chosen for a reason.
        "Chosen . . . that we should be holy and without blame before him in love" (v. 4).

4. We were chosen to be His own.
    "Unto the adoption of children by Jesus Christ to himself" (v. 5).
5. We were chosen for His glory.
    "To the praise of the glory of his grace" (v. 6).

II. We were divinely redeemed through grace.
1. Which has brought us the forgiveness of sins.
    "The forgiveness of sin, according to the riches of his grace" (v. 7).
2. Which has united us to Christ (vv. 8-10).
    "That . . . he might gather together in one all things in Christ" (v. 10).
3. Which has made all believers one body.
    "He might gather together in one all things in Christ, both which are in heaven, and which are on earth; even in him" (v. 10).
4. Which has made us His holy heritage.
    Greek: "We were made a heritage" (v. 11).
5. Which has brought glory to His name (v. 12).

III. We were divinely sealed in grace.
1. The Holy Spirit has sealed us.
    "Ye were sealed with that holy Spirit of promise" (v. 13).
2. The Holy Spirit is God's promise He will complete His work in us.
    "Which is the earnest of our inheritance until the redemption of the purchased possession" (v. 14).
    Earnest means a guarantee or down payment. As the engagement ring is a promise that the marriage will be consummated, so the Holy Spirit is the promise our salvation will be completed.
3. The sealing is for God's glory.
    "Unto the praise of his glory" (v. 14).

Conclusion:

Salvation in the New Testament is spoken of in three time sequences: I have been saved; I am now being saved; and I shall be saved.

Only part of that has been completed in the believer. The consummation of our salvation will be our glorification, when we are made in the likeness of Christ (1 John 3:2; 1 Cor. 15:49).

But it is all by God's grace: chosen, redeemed, and sealed by God's grace.

---

1. Walter B. Knight, *Knight's Master Book of New Illustrations* (Grand Rapids: Wm. B. Eerdmans Publishing Company, 1956), p. 262. From *Christian Digest*. Used by permission.

56
Them's Good Words

Scripture: *Matthew 11:28-30*

Introduction:

According to a story told by F. W. Boreham, three slaves sat around a fire late one evening along the Red River. There were two women and Uncle Tom. It had been a long, difficult day, and they were bone tired.

Uncle Tom ground some corn for the evening meal, and the two women baked some corn cakes. Tom then opened his Bible and began to read.

One of the women asked what book it was Tom was reading, and he replied, "The Bible."

"What kind of Book is that?" she asked. "Read a piece of it to me."

Tom then turned to these words of Jesus, "Come unto me, all ye that labour and are heavy laden, and I will give you rest."

The woman listened intently to Tom as he read. And when he had finished, she exclaimed, "Them's good words! Who says 'em?"

"Why, woman," Tom exclaimed, "those are the words of Jesus."

Nothing that Jesus said means more to weary, struggling believers than these blessed and comforting words from Matthew's Gospel. Millions of us affirm with the old slave woman that "Them's good words!"

Let me suggest several reasons why these are good words.

I. They are good words because they invite us to Jesus. "Come unto me" (v. 28).

II. They are good words because they encourage us. "All ye that labour and are heavy laden, and I will give you rest" (v. 28).

III. They are good words because they comfort us. "I will give you rest . . . ye shall find rest unto your souls" (vv. 28-29).

IV. They are good words because they instruct us. "Take my yoke . . . learn of me . . . I am meek and lowly . . . my yoke is easy . . . my burden is light" (vv. 29-30).

V. They are good words because they strengthen us. "Heavy laden . . . rest . . . take my yoke . . . ye shall find rest" (vv. 28-29).

Conclusion:

In his book *A Bunch of Everlastings*, F. W. Boreham relates that years ago England's Queen Victoria had the architect Marochetti carve a memorial to young Princess Elizabeth. It is located in a chapel at Newport on the Isle of Wight.

Carved from marble, there lies the image of the beautiful, dead, young princess. Her eyes are closed, and her lips are parted just a little as though it were her last sigh.

One arm of the princess is upon her waist and the other has fallen to her side. Her dainty little hand is half open, and her head is gently resting upon an old, open Bible. Her long curls fall carelessly across the page.

But beneath the curls can be clearly read the words of the Savior: "Come unto me, all ye that labour and are heavy laden, and I will give you rest" (v. 28).

To whomever these words of Jesus have been read, whether to slaves, princesses, kings and queens, or common folks like you and me, each of us has affirmed, "Them's good words."

57
Two Views of the Cross

Scripture: 1 Corinthians 1:18

Introduction:

Death by crucifixion was not one of the methods of execution used by the Jews. They used strangulation, burning, stoning, or beheading. They left crucifixion to the less-civilized nations of the world.

Death by crucifixion was of Phoenician origin. It was later adopted by the Romans and improved on, and the Romans used it a great deal in the first three centuries when they dominated the ancient world.

Thousands of men have died on crosses. Five centuries before Jesus, Darius, the Mede, overran Persia, and when the dust had settled, he had crucified three thousand captives of war.

Three centuries before Jesus, Alexander the Great ravaged the ancient world, and when he took the ancient city of Tyre, Alexander crucified two thousand people before the city was brought under his dominion. One ancient historian said that the crosses stood on Tyre's barren hillsides more numerous than the masts of ships in Tyre's harbor.

Another historian, in describing Titus's conquest of Jerusalem in AD 71, wrote that there was not sufficient wood around Jerusalem to build crosses for Titus.

Although crucifixion was not uncommon in the ancient world, the crucifixion of Jesus Christ was different from all others. On the cross, in fulfillment of Isaiah's prophecy, Jesus "was numbered with the transgressors" and "with his stripes we are healed."

Paul tells us in this text that there are two views of the cross—and only two views—held by mankind everywhere.

I. The absurdity of the cross.

"For the preaching of the cross is to them that perish foolishness" (v. 18). The word *foolishness* is *moria* which gives us the word *moron*.

1. The message of the shed blood by which we are saved is foolishness to those who are perishing (vv. 18,23).
2. The simplicity of the way of salvation is foolishness to those who are perishing (vv. 18,23).

II. The adequacy of the cross.

"But unto us which are saved it is the power of God" (vv. 18,24). The word *power* is *dunamis* which gives us the word *dynamite*.

1. The cross is adequate in redeeming power (Heb. 7:25).
2. The cross is adequate in changing power (2 Cor. 5:17).

Conclusion:

The center of our faith is the cross of Jesus and the empty tomb. Doubters and scoffers look at the cross and say, "It is foolishness—an absurdity." But those of us who are believers look at the cross and say, "It is adequate—sufficient for all our needs."

Texan Jack Brown wrote a book about his life titled *Monkey on My Back*. It is Brown's testimony, which I heard on two occasions, about his misspent life and his conversion to the Savior.

Brown spent seventeen years in prison. He was in county jails for three years. And he was on the run from the police for years. He served time in five penitentiaries and was a dope addict for years. Brown even spent time on death row.

Brown told me he had no idea how much money he had stolen or taken by fraud or forgery. He also said that at one time he and his friends got $255,000 in cash from a doctor they were blackmailing.

But God got hold of Jack Brown's life. Through the prayers of his wife and mother, Brown was gloriously saved, and his life was radically changed.

Many of us can give a similar testimony. Although most of

us have not lived outside the law as Brown did, we joyously testify that Jesus intercepted our lives and changed them.

Contrary to what the unsaved world says about the cross, we testify that it is totally adequate.

58
When Life Presents Its Bill

Scripture: Judges 1:5-7

Introduction:

Walter B. Knight told about a lawyer who once lived in Scotland. He rented a horse from a poor man and so abused the horse that it died. The poor man insisted that the lawyer pay him for his horse.

The lawyer didn't deny his guilt and told the poor man he was willing to pay. "But," he said, "at the moment I'm a little short of money and would appreciate some time."

The poor farmer, a gracious and understanding man, didn't mind giving the lawyer some time. Since the lawyer insisted he could not pay any time soon, the farmer told the lawyer simply to set his own time when he would pay for the horse.

Being a slick operator, the lawyer drew up the papers stating that he would pay for the horse on judgment day.

Knowing he had been taken, the poor man went to court and asked the judge to examine the note.

After the judge had examined the note, he agreed that the note was perfectly legal and then told the lawyer, "The day of judgment has come. Pay the man for his horse."

There comes a time when life presents its bill to be paid. God will let us live exactly as we want to live, and we may go along months or even years when God says nothing to us about how we are living. But this doesn't mean God has forgotten, and the day will surely come when life presents its bill.

This is what this text says. After the Israelites moved out of the wilderness into Canaan, the tribes of Judah and Simeon encountered stiff opposition at Bezek. The town soon fell into their hands, and they took King Adoni-bezek captive.

Then they did a strange thing. It is the only time in the Bible that such an occurance appears, so far as I know. After capturing King Adoni-bezek, they cut off his thumbs and his big toes. After the mutilation he was no longer able to fight and lead his men. The proud, wicked, powerful king was reduced to a weakling.

There are some lessons we can learn from the experience of this pagan Canaanite.

I. Sin will catch up with us.
    1.   We can run from God.
       "But Adoni-bezek fled" (v. 6).
    2.   But we can't hide from God.
       "And they pursued after him, and caught him" (v. 6).
    3.   The day of reckoning comes.
       "And cut off his thumbs and his great toes" (v. 6).
II. We reap what we sow.
    1.   It is a natural law.
       When the farmer plants corn, he reaps corn. When he plants wheat, he reaps wheat. Reaping what we sow is a natural law operative in the universe.
    2.   It is a spiritual law.
       God required that Adoni-bezek pay for his sins in like kind: "And Adoni-bezek said, Three-score and ten kings, having their thumbs and their great toes cut off, gathered their meat under my table: as I have done, so God hath requited me" (v. 7). (See also Gal. 6:7-8.)
    3.   It is a just law.
       There is no complaint from Adoni-bezek about the treatment he received. The passage intimates that Adoni-bezek felt his punishment was fair.
    4.   It is a redemptive law.
       "So God hath required me" (v. 7). Adoni-bezek was a Canaanite. He didn't have the spiritual background the Jews had. But he understood that the punishment which he had suffered was divine punishment for his sins. One cannot help but wonder

if this confession of Adoni-bezek, "God hath requit-
ed me," is a confession of his faith.

Conclusion:
R. L. Middleton in his book *Accents of Life*, told about a new
family that moved into a farming community. They weren't a
Christian family and didn't attend church on Sunday. They
worked their crops on the Lord's Day as though it were just
another day of the week.

A Christian who lived nearby invited the father to attend
Sunday School at their country church, but the farmer boasted
that he could get along all right without the church or without
honoring the Lord's Day.

"My crops will be as good as yours," he told his neighbor,
"even if I work them on Sunday and don't go to church."

And the Christian neighbor replied, "That may be true. But
you need to remember that God doesn't settle his accounts in
October."

The farmer told the truth. The day will eventually come
when life presents its bill to be paid.

59
Will Jesus Come Again?

Scripture: 2 Peter 3:1-13

Introduction:
Confederate President Jefferson Davis relieved General Joseph Johnston as commander of the army of Tennessee when
Union General William T. Sherman began his destructive
march across Georgia. Davis thought Johnston was too cau-
tious as the general retreated before Sherman's troops.

General John Bell Hood took command of the army of
Tennessee in 1864 and unsuccessfully resisted Sherman's at-
tack on Atlanta.

Hood retreated from Atlanta toward Tennessee hoping that

Sherman would follow him. If he could trap Sherman's army in the mountains, he thought he could beat him.

General Sherman ordered Lieutenant Corse and a contingent of troops to march against Allatoona. From Kennesaw Mountain, Sherman could clearly see the smoke of battle and hear the faint sounds of the cannons at Allatoona.

Sherman's flag officer read a message to Sherman that was being wigwagged to the general from Corse at Allatoona. It read, "Corse is here."

Responding to Corse's message, Sherman sent to the lieutenant the encouraging word, "Hold the fort, I am coming."

When this incident was later related to Evangelist P. P. Bliss, he wrote the words to the well-known hymn: "Hold the Fort."

> Ho, my commrades! see the signal/Waving in the sky! Reinforcements now appearing,/Victory is nigh./"Hold the fort, for I am coming,"/Jesus signals still;/Wave the answer back to heaven,/"By thy grace we will."

In Peter's message to the struggling first-century Christians, he tells us that Jesus is coming again, and we are to stay by the stuff and be faithful to Him until He comes.

Although Jesus' coming may be delayed, we are not to listen to the scoffers who say that the delay is evidence He will not come at all. In answer to their scoffing question, "Will Jesus come again?" believers are to answer with Peter's promise: "But the day of the Lord will come" (v. 10).

I. The certainty of His coming (2 Pet. 3:10).
    1. The certainty of His coming was taught by Jesus (Mark 14:62; Matt. 16:27).
    2. The certainty of His coming was believed by the apostles (Acts 1:10-11).
    3. The certainty of His coming was preached by Paul (1 Thess. 4:16; Col. 3:4).
    4. The certainty of His coming was believed by the church (1 Thess. 4:13-18).

II. The time of His coming (2 Pet. 3:4,8,12).
    1. The time is known only to God (Matt. 24:36,42; Mark 13:32-33).
    2. The time will be when least expected (Mark 13:32-37; Matt. 24:36-44).
    3. The time may be at any time (Jas. 5:7-9; Phil. 4:5).

4. The time will be self-evident (Matt. 24:23-28).
III. The manner of His coming (2 Pet. 3:10).
   1. It will be personal (Acts 1:11).
   2. It will be sudden (2 Pet. 3:10; Rev. 22:20).
   3. It will be calamitous for some (2 Pet. 3:9-13; Matt. 25:30-33,41,46).
   4. It will be victorious for others (2 Pet. 3:13-14; Matt. 25:33-34,46).
IV. The proper attitude toward His coming (2 Pet. 3:11-12).
   1. We must expect it (Mark 13:35-37; 2 Pet. 3:12; Matt. 25:1-13).
   2. We must be prepared (2 Pet. 3:11; Matt. 25:1-13).
   3. We must be faithful (Matt. 25:14-30; 2 Pet. 3:17-18).
   4. We must be patient (2 Pet. 3:8-12; Heb. 10:36).
   5. We must be holy (2 Pet. 3:13-14).
   6. We must be busy (Matt. 24:45-51).

Conclusion:

The great theologian and preacher G. Campbell Morgan said that the certainty of Christ's coming made his life possible. He said he never put his head on his pillow without thinking that Jesus might come before he awoke. Campbell added that he never turned to his work without thinking Jesus might interrupt it with His sudden appearance.

And this must be our attitude as believers in an age that mockingly asks: "Will Jesus come again?"

60
Your Golden Opportunity

Scripture: Mark 10:13-31

Introduction:

Clarence Macartney in his book *Macartney's Illustrations* tells about an old Saxon king whose kingdom was divided by rebellion. Calling together his army, the king set out for the distant provinces to quell the insurrection. Returning to his palace, he placed a lighted candle in his castle and then instructed one of his servants to tell the rebels that if they would surrender and take an oath of loyalty while the candle was still burning, they would be pardoned.

The messenger did as he was bidden. He carried the good news to the offenders that mercy was available as long as the candle burned. He urged them to seize their golden opportunity before it was too late!

When Jesus came into the world, Almighty God lighted a candle. This candle of opportunity burns brightly today, and God says to us through Jesus Christ His Son: "While the candle burns, you may be saved. This is your golden opportunity to enter the kingdom of God. Don't wait until it's too late."

Long ago during the ministry of Jesus, a young man came to the master asking the question, "Good Master, what shall I do that I may inherit eternal life?" (v. 17).

He wanted to know how to seize his golden opportunity. And Jesus told him what was involved in entering the kingdom of God.

    I. The way to enter the kingdom of God.
        1. Jesus used a child to show us the way (v. 14).
        2. Jesus said we must have the faith of a little child (v. 15).
        3. Jesus shows us how He will respond to childlike faith (v. 16).
    II. The hindrances to entering the kingdom of God.
        1. Pride is a hindrance (vv. 19-20).
        2. Self-centeredness is a hindrance (vv. 21-25).
    III. The blessings of entering the kingdom.
        1. Blessings in this life (vv. 28-30).
        2. Blessings in the life to come (vv. 30-31).

Conclusion:

When Teddy Roosevelt was commanding his Rough Riders in Cuba during the Spanish-American War, he heard that Clara Barton, the founder of the Red Cross, was on the island. When Roosevelt heard that Barton had secured a supply of sweets for some invalids for whom she was caring, Roosevelt asked her to sell some to him for his sick men. But Miss Barton refused Roosevelt's request. When Roosevelt assured her that he was willing to pay for the sweets himself, Miss Barton told him that they were not for sale but that he could have them only for the asking.

Your golden opportunity to enter the kingdom of God lies before you. And it is yours simply for the asking.